Praise for

## THE ILLUSION OF
# MONEY

'*The Illusion of Money* is like a 'get out of jail free' *Monopoly* card when it comes to the subject of money. If you read this book while staying fully present and actually do the exercises and stick with it, you will discover a real space inside you . . . where prosperity comes from. And your life will be changed for good. Plus, you will laugh a lot because Kyle is a very funny person.'

— **Dr Christiane Northrup**, *New York Times* bestselling author of *Women's Bodies, Women's Wisdom* and *Goddesses Never Age*

'Kyle Cease is one of the most brilliant, hilarious, and masterful teachers today. His powerful work will help you get out of your own way so you can create a big, beautiful life beyond your wildest dreams. This book is a must-read (and read again!).'

— **Kris Carr**, # 1 *New York Times* bestselling author of *Crazy Sexy Juice*

'A master class on living the life you were born to live through loving yourself, filled with powerful metaphors, profound wisdom, and lots of great humor. Loved it!'

— **Mike Dooley**, *New York Times* bestselling author of *Infinite Possibilities* and *A Beginner's Guide to the Universe*

'What if the pursuit of money wasn't the root of all evil, but it didn't do anything to make you happy either? In this profound book, Kyle elegantly transforms one of the biggest sources of stress to a higher perspective where money is the by-product of learning to access the creative genius that lives inside each and every one of us.'

— **Dave Asprey**, CEO and founder of Bulletproof and *New York Times* bestselling author of *The Bulletproof Diet*

'Physical resources and clock time may be limited, but imagination and creativity are potentially boundless. How can we fulfill that potential? How can we move beyond our self-imposed limitations to enter the realm of Leonardo DaVinci, Marie Curie, Nikola Tesla, and Elon Musk? Kyle Cease abides in this realm, and he shows how you can, too. With humor, wisdom, and verve, he guides us to discover the power of awareness, thereby liberating new dimensions of abundance, freedom, and joy. Bravo!'

— **Michael J. Gelb**, founder and president of The High Performance Learning Center and bestselling author of *How to Think Like Leonardo da Vinci: Seven Steps to Genius Every Day*

'In this motivational, insightful, must-read book, Cease helps us to release our obsession with money and shift to a place beyond money by tapping into our genius levels to discover that we are the source of everything, thus bringing our gifts and our passions to the world to receive massive, true abundance and live the life of our dreams.'

— **Anita Moorjani**, *New York Times* bestselling author of *Dying to Be Me* and *What If This Is Heaven*

'*The Illusion of Money* is a total game changer. In it, Kyle helps people to overcome some of their biggest limiting beliefs around money and invites them to discover what true abundance really is.'

— **Lewis Howes**, host of The School of Greatness podcast and *New York Times* bestselling author of *The School of Greatness*

'Kyle Cease raises the bar with this book; forcing us to think outside the box of social conditioning to redefine the way we prosper in a modern spiritual era.'

— **Matt Kahn**, bestselling author of *Everything Is Here to Help You*

'With the rising consciousness of humanity that is upon us, it is paramount that we learn the skills of stewarding our lives with grace and inspired flow. We are meant to thrive on every level of life, and integrated financial abundance is crucial to our sustainable awakening, both personally and culturally. Kyle captures the spirit of money and the role its energy has in our evolution. True success and spirituality merge here in *The Illusion of Money* for the greater good. Thank you, Kyle. You are a gift.'

— **Dr Sue Morter**, founder and CEO of Morter Institute for BioEnergetics and bestselling author of *The Energy Codes*

'Kyle is going to cause you to laugh your way into understanding your potential that you have locked up in you. I'm going to introduce him to everyone I know.'

— **Bob Proctor**, entrepreneur, speaker, coach, teacher of *The Secret* and bestselling author of *The ABCs of Success*

'Kyle says things that are true but in a funny way. In some people that is called a comedian, but with him it's a heart-opening experience that rises your spirit and helps you remember the meaning of it all.'

— **Biet Simkin**, spiritual teacher and author of *Don't Just Sit There!*

# THE ILLUSION OF
# MONEY

## Also by Kyle Cease

*I HOPE I SCREW THIS UP: How Falling in Love*
*with Your Fears Can Change the World*

# THE ILLUSION OF
# MONEY

## WHY CHASING MONEY IS
## STOPPING YOU FROM RECEIVING IT

# KYLE CEASE

**HAY HOUSE**

Carlsbad, California • New York City
London • Sydney • New Delhi

**Published in the United Kingdom by:**
Hay House UK Ltd, The Sixth Floor, Watson House,
54 Baker Street, London W1U 7BU
Tel: +44 (0)20 3927 7290; Fax: +44 (0)20 3927 7291
www.hayhouse.co.uk

**Published in the United States of America by:**
Hay House Inc., PO Box 5100, Carlsbad, CA 92018-5100
Tel: (1) 760 431 7695 or (800) 654 5126
Fax: (1) 760 431 6948 or (800) 650 5115; www.hayhouse.com

**Published in Australia by:**
Hay House Australia Ltd, 18/36 Ralph St, Alexandria NSW 2015
Tel: (61) 2 9669 4299; Fax: (61) 2 9669 4144; www.hayhouse.com.au

**Published in India by:**
Hay House Publishers India, Muskaan Complex, Plot No.3, B-2,
Vasant Kunj, New Delhi 110 070
Tel: (91) 11 4176 1620; Fax: (91) 11 4176 1630; www.hayhouse.co.in

Text © Kyle Cease, 2019

*Cover design:* Jervais Dionne and Dan McKim
*Interior design:* Nick C. Welch

The moral rights of the author have been asserted.

The information given in this book should not be treated as a
substitute for professional medical advice; always consult a medical
practitioner. Any use of information in this book is at the reader's
discretion and risk. Neither the author nor the publisher can be held
responsible for any loss, claim or damage arising out of the use, or
misuse, of the suggestions made, the failure to take medical advice or
for any material on third-party websites.

A catalogue record for this book is available from the British Library.

Tradepaper ISBN: 978-1-78817-324-7
Hardback ISBN: 978-1-4019-5744-5
E-book ISBN: 978-1-78817-566-1

Printed and bound in Great Britain by
TJ Books Limited, Padstow, Cornwall

# CONTENTS

# FOREWORD

Our relationship to money begins pre-birth. Its seeds are sown in the psyches of our ancestors burgeoning forth to enter ours across many generations. Families develop an archetypal blueprint around money and pass on values and belief systems that are profoundly powerful, albeit unconscious. Our ideologies around money influence us far more than we can ever imagine. In fact, I would go as far as to say that our relationship to money is both a key influencer and indicator of our sense of worth, purpose, and place in this world.

Parents in particular are zealously obsessed with their children's financial well-being. Guised as "success," most parents claim that they desire this for their children because they believe that this is the pathway to their happiness. Consciously or unconsciously, parents, like us all, have associated money with all things good: peace, beauty, harmony, and the ubiquitous treasure called happiness. It is because we have tied success, i.e. financial well-being, to an internal state of utopia that parents let themselves off the hook and allow themselves to push their children to achieve this coveted prize called "success" at all costs. In the name of love, they push and pressure themselves and their children toward being "the best," little realizing that there is no scientific consensus on what it means to truly be successful.

To chase money is the way we have all been raised. We have all grown up observing this highly toxic dependence on money: happy when we have it and stressed when we don't. We have grown up absorbing an ideology that money is something scarce and to be coveted. We are raised to see it as this elusive prize that only the very fortunate get to win. Our life's mission, then, is to accumulate loads of it at all costs. It is here, in our early conditioning around money and its implicit association with happiness that creates our tragic dependence on it.

What if we grew up in a different way, where money was conditioned into our psyches in a radically novel manner? Instead of believing it was this coveted, scarce commodity, we were conditioned to believe it was not only freely available and abundant but also as unrelated to our happiness. Wouldn't we breathe easier? Wouldn't we take greater risks and allow for greater change in our lives? The truth is that we have been raised to project all sorts of magical properties onto money which then creates our hapless craving of it. We truly believe we will be better humans if we had more of it. Due to this anxious and almost infantile dependence on it, our lives are betrothed to it. Money then becomes our primary bedfellow, where we mentally enslave ourselves to its presence or absence, forever oscillating to its tune.

Every financially prosperous person will admit that money does not buy happiness. Their testimonies fall on deaf ears. Why? Because we see them with their fancy shoes and yachts and project happiness onto their life situations. "How can they not be happy lying on their private beach?" we wonder. Yet, every wealthy person will attest that their money and the possessions it buys does not fill their inner void, nor does it deliver any enduring sense of meaning or purpose.

So how do we change our relationship to something so deeply ingrained in our collective psyches as money? How do we learn a new way of relating to it so that it doesn't own us anymore? This is where this phenomenal book by my dear friend Kyle Cease comes in. This book will show you how to extricate from the dysfunctional relationship we have created with money and how to find true purpose, peace, and happiness regardless of its presence or absence. Do you know what this spells for me? Freedom.

Kyle's own personal liberation from money resounds through all the pages of this book. It is clear that he has entered a space of empowered detachment from money and reached a place where he is no longer defined by its existence. He teaches us to touch our inner core of wholeness and abide here with empowerment to such a degree that we no longer need to seek to fill ourselves with anything—money or otherwise—outside of ourselves.

Kyle's eloquent and brilliant book teaches us to discover our inner alignment within which we discover an elevated sense of abundance and joy. He offers us a path out of our dependence on money and into a state of inner transcendence where all things external whither away. Kyle's words are a beacon in today's achievement-oriented world, shining the way for a new way of being human where authenticity replaces achievement, sovereignty replaces success, compassion replaces craving, and peace replaces paucity.

Financial freedom is not something to be craved. It is not something to be sought or achieved. It cannot, for one reason only: it doesn't exist outside of us. It all exists within. Financial well-being is a state of mind. Kyle shows us how to achieve this and sustain this. His words will allow you to transcend all your fears around money and find a way to radiate with an abiding sense of inner wealth, of which money is only one piece.

Take heed . . . you are about to liberate yourself.

— Dr. Shefali Tsabary, clinical psychologist and *New York Times* best-selling author of *The Awakened Family,* www.drshefali.com

# INTRODUCTION

I did a little research and found that only a small percentage of people actually read the introduction of a book, so know that you are an extremely special person who I like more than the people who didn't read this part. I'm joking. I like everyone slightly different amounts based on their mustache length. Seriously though, I imagine that someone who reads the introduction of a book is also the type of person who actually finishes the books they pick up—so it looks like we're in it for the long haul together. I want to take this extra time that we have here to share a few additional things about this book with you that might help you get even more out of it.

First off, I am extremely excited to share this book with you. With as much humility as possible, I truly believe that if you read with an open mind and an open heart, the concepts in this book could completely transform multiple aspects of your life. In addition to other potential benefits, it's my hope that this book will expose the unconscious preoccupation with money that society has programmed into you and help to liberate you from it. You are an infinite creative being who has been living within the confines of an unconscious world for most of your life—it's time to discover what real freedom actually feels like.

I want to let you know that I'm not going to help you just feel better about money or create financial freedom by showing you strategies to make more money. More money will likely be a by-product of what you discover about yourself in this book, but it is not the goal or the reason behind it. You can't put a fire out by pouring gasoline on it. You can't cure an addiction by giving someone more of what they are addicted to. To truly move beyond our mental ties to money, we need to get to root of things and bring awareness to the illusion that has been living inside of our bodies for decades.

This entire book is about raising your awareness. Awareness is everything. Awareness is what allows Stevie Wonder to reach out and grab a hit song from some invisible dimension. Awareness is what causes Ellen DeGeneres to bring through a comedic vibration that connects with the world. Awareness is what helps Elon Musk receive the ideas to do all the crazy shit he does. Those people are no different from you or me; they just have an awareness of higher possibilities that gives them access to all their incredible talents. When our awareness is small, we're blind to the unimaginable inspiration that is available to us and become focused on the struggle to survive. When we *raise* our awareness, the magic of life starts to show up and the abundance that is all around us comes into focus.

I'll speak more about this later in the book, but the process of raising your awareness can feel exciting and expansive—and it can also be challenging at times because it often involves letting go of old, familiar, habitual beliefs. If you experience uncomfortable moments while reading, know that they are just growing pains that will lead to a more expanded and freer you. It also might be indigestion.

Up until now, many of us have seen money as a thing that we need to control or conquer somehow—but I want to offer you the opportunity to begin seeing your relationship with money the way that you would see your relationship with a person. If you are in a relationship with someone who is overly needy, controlling, fearful, anxious, unworthy, or possessive, that person will probably start to become extremely unattractive to you and you'll start avoiding them. If you're in a relationship with someone who is confident, carefree, playful, appreciative, and generous, then you'll probably be more attracted to that person and will want to hang out with them more. So if you feel needy, controlling, fearful, anxious, unworthy, or possessive over money, money will probably avoid you even more. If you're appreciative when money comes to you, confident in your ability to create abundance, and generous with the money you have, money will probably start to want to be around you more.

There will be countless opportunities in this book to look at money in a different way and to discover how the issues we have with money often mirror things within ourselves that we haven't fully seen or accepted. Most of the world is in the practice of chasing money so they can use it as a Band-Aid for the pain and insecurity that they have inside. This book is about undoing the illusion that money will fix your life. Money is not what we really want. What we want is freedom, joy, creativity, love, connection, community, energy, health, contribution, peace. No matter how much you accumulate, money will never bring you those things all by itself. The truth is, you don't need money to create any of those things anyway. Through the process of reading this book, you'll learn how to cultivate the experience of all those positive things with or without money. (Oh, and once you have all those things and don't even care about money, money will probably show up all over the place, but don't tell your ego that or it will start trying to create all those amazing things just so it can get money, which doesn't work as well.)

My entire life and career have been about discovering how to listen to my inspired callings instead of the circumstances or the people around me. I have been so fortunate to live the principles in this book and discover an incredibly abundant life—both internally and externally. What I'll offer here are the principles and ideas that my team and I have used to create a heart-centered business that has continually doubled each year in revenue, reach, and impact. Take what resonates with you; leave what doesn't. What I'm sharing are concepts that I've discovered through my personal, firsthand experiences that have shifted me into a world of more results while bringing in more play, more freedom, more ease, and more fulfillment. This is not something I read in a book somewhere. This is my life.

So, you're here. You've shown up and taken the first step toward discovering a life beyond money and a way of being that accesses your full abundance in every moment. I know that as more of us begin to move past our conditioned beliefs and connect with ourselves on a deeper level, we will help make this a better planet for ourselves and our children. I'm honored that you are here and honored to do this work with you.

That's the end of the book—the rest is just a bibliography.

Just kidding, there's a shitload more.

Here it comes . . .

# CHAPTER 1

# WELCOME TO THE ILLUSION

Imagine if Michael Jordan, at the height of his legendary basketball career, got amnesia and completely forgot who he was. After coming to, he struggles to get a day job, finds a mediocre relationship, starts watching a lot of TV, and gets used to living an ordinary, unfulfilling life. In this alternate reality (with many different obvious plot holes) he's now walking around thinking he's an average guy and trying to figure out how to make ends meet while getting more and more unhappy with his life.

If you met him, you'd probably be obsessed with trying to help him remember that he's one of the greatest basketball players who ever lived. You'd be doing everything in your power to get him on the court so he could realize how amazing he actually is. But imagine him completely believing and defending that he's just an ordinary guy—and explaining to you that he has bills to pay and he can't just spend his time chasing some dream of playing basketball all day.

You'd be going crazy listening to him complain about how hard it is to get by because you know about the hundreds of millions of dollars and total fulfillment he's missing out on by not trusting that he has this insane talent and value that he could bring to the world. Every time you'd go to the Applebee's he now works at, you'd be trying to convince him to leave and do this thing you know he's amazing at, but he'd remind you about how, if he stays there another two years, they'll make him assistant manager—and that he needs that kind of security in his life.

You're sitting there, trying to show him who he actually is, because he has no idea, and he's angrily defending this new, small life because he can't see what's beyond it from his limited perspective.

This is how I see most people. No matter who I talk to, they seem to have amnesia about who they really are.

I may not know you personally, so I don't know your story or what you do for a living, but here's what I do know: you are a brilliant, creative genius. I don't need to know anything about you to know that. I'm not trying to pump you up or make you feel special—it's a fact. And don't try to argue with me about it—first, because this is a book and I'm not actually in front of you, so you'd just be talking to a book, and more importantly, because it's the truth. Every voice in your head that tells you anything other than that is a lie you've been told by the world that has made you forget what you actually are.

After working with thousands and thousands of people from all over the planet, I've come to learn that every single person has the exact same level of unique brilliance in them, we all just access it in different amounts. How much we're accessing our brilliance depends only on how much we're attached to the limited story that cuts us off from it. If you could find a way, for just a second, to let go of your limited story that is telling you that you're not a genius . . . BOOM—your genius would show up instantly.

So every single one of us is holding on to an idea of ourselves that is only a tiny fraction of what we can truly become. In letting go of that idea, it doesn't mean we're all going to be able to dunk from the free-throw line like Jordan, but it does mean that each one of us has a totally unique gift that is waiting to come through in an equally badass way. But when we're living in our amnesia and believing our small story, we spend our lives stressing about things that would be completely taken care of if we stepped into the magic of what we actually are.

The reason this book is called *The Illusion of Money* is because money is one of the *biggest* excuses we give ourselves for why we can't follow our highest calling and step into what we are meant to become. If you want to be a writer, a painter, an entrepreneur, or anything else, but spend all your time working at a job you don't like just because it pays the bills, that's using money as an excuse to disqualify all your unlimited talents and creativity. If you want to travel the world but don't because you think you can't afford it, that's using money as an excuse to not connect to the infinite possibility and synchronicity that is available when you take the first step and show up. I get that there are details about those types of situations that your mind might be pointing out as examples of how those things might not work—if any arguments like that came up, realize that's the limited part of you arguing for its limitations. If you stopped arguing for your limitations, you'd start to see how it's all possible instead of how it's impossible. There are a million different ways that we let our illusional set of limitations around money keep us from following the excited ideas and dreams that we have—and it's costing us our life.

After twenty-five years as a successful comedian, actor, transformational speaker, author, and junior-league amateur bowler, I've experienced many, many times how chasing money is not an effective way to create an abundant and fulfilling life. For years, I had the experience of taking gigs because the money was mentally exciting and then being completely exhausted because it wasn't in alignment with my highest calling. One of the moments that I felt most alive was when I left my comedy career at its peak to become a transformational speaker so I could share this deeper part of myself with the world. I left tons of guaranteed money and so-called security for a complete unknown. It was terrifying—but what was on the other side of that terror was a completely different life that is not only more abundant financially, but has more freedom, more ease, more passion, more impact, and more joy.

I'm not writing this book because I'm trying to sell this idea to you; I'm writing this book because I've actually experienced what happens when you let go of a lifetime of attachment to money and achievement—and step into a life of actual alignment and listening to whatever that thing is that's beating our hearts. That thing doesn't give a shit about money. Life doesn't care about what you have in your bank account. It wants to grow and learn and connect and love and create and play.

This book is an invitation for you to let go of the part of you that is trying to get results and doesn't feel worthy. You don't need results; you *are* the result. This entire universe had to do everything it did for billions of years for you to exist right now. You're the point of this whole thing—there's nothing you need to do to prove yourself.

I realize that many books about money are *only* about the results. I know that it might sound backward to suggest that you don't need to chase results to experience abundance, but what if chasing results is actually the thing that's keeping us from experiencing real abundance? What if we're starting to understand that believing we need any specific result is just a remnant of an old paradigm that thinks the results are more important than us? The results aren't the magic; *we're* the magic. We're the source of any result that comes into our lives, so we can stop falling in love with results and start falling in love with *ourselves*.

That feels good, doesn't it? To let all of that chasing and needing to achieve drop for a second and realize that you're here, you've made it. There's nothing else required. Everything beyond the fact of your existence is just a bonus. Life is a playground.

Take a second, close your eyes, and feel the part of you that is just happy to be alive.

If you actually did that instead of just continuing to read like most people, you might have felt more connected to your body and to the whole of your being as you relaxed a little (which is why now is a great opportunity to go back and do that exercise instead of skipping it). It seems as if 99 percent of our creative energy has been spent trying to hold together this illusion of limitation and unworthiness—the moment we stop holding it together, we unlock an entirely new dimension of abilities and freedom.

This is why I find the phrase "trying to keep it all together" so fascinating. What are we trying to keep together? If you have to try to keep something together, maybe it's not supposed to be there. Maybe what you're trying to keep together is an old way of being that doesn't fit anymore. Maybe your limitations and feelings of unworthiness are finally being outgrown. Maybe you can let it all go and allow an entirely new you to show up. An architect can't build a brand-new hotel right on top of an existing old one—he needs to demolish the old one, clear it out of the way, and prepare the ground for a new one. What if all it takes is to let the plates fall and give yourself the space to discover the worthiness and freedom that you actually are? In that space, new aligned circumstances will start to show up in your life because they're no longer being blocked with a mental illusion of your own limitation.

Even though this awareness of the unlimited possibilities of life is available all the time, almost everyone in the world spends the majority of their day living in their heads, stuck in their mental entanglement with a limited story that stops them from truly connecting with themselves and the abundance that is available to them.

For example, think about how much of each day you spend thinking of things that you can't control—like what a politician said, what someone said about you, something you have to do later, what your parents think about you, what a sports team did, what's going to happen in the future, or what happened in the past. What percentage of each day is your mind consumed with something that you actually can't control at all? Really stop and think about it. What would your answer be? Fifty percent of the day? Seventy-five? Ninety? Feel free to use fractions instead. You could also try the metric system if you want to discover how many centimeters per day you are worrying about something you can't control.

When you finally release the things you can't control and allow yourself to not be consumed with pointless worrying, what do you think you will make space for? What do you think would be on the other side of that? What would be possible? If you had a year of being free from your entanglement with temporary, mental distractions, what do you think would happen?

This is where your Michael Jordan . . . or Oprah Winfrey or Gandhi or Steve Jobs or Elvis shows up. I guarantee you that all the people we consider to be the greatest in the world, in their moments of highest creativity, were not focused on anything other than their connection to themselves and the moment, and they weren't keeping alive a story of unworthiness or doubt about what is possible.

So this book isn't really about money; it's about connecting to the holy-shit version of yourself that is here to change the planet. That doesn't mean you need to be a famous athlete or business owner or TV personality—life's highest calling for you might be to relax and live in a simple, humble way that allows your presence to powerfully impact each person you come into contact with. Either way, in this place of connection to yourself, you will discover how powerfully life is waiting to create through you when you are willing to let go of your constant drive to fix a story that you perceive as broken. Our endless desire for money (or fear of money) is often really a desire to be safe or to be seen by the world. This book is about eliminating the need to seek safety through the illusion of money and learning to see ourselves for the perfection that we are, beginning to bring our creative power to the world in an authentic way, and allowing ourselves to receive massive, true abundance in all areas as a by-product.

You will discover that, on the other side of this mental illusion of money, there is a powerful guidance system that just needs you to get out of your own way. You have infinite callings, next steps, ideas, and more all waiting for you—and your job is to become receptive to that guidance. Your job is to co-create with the moment . . . and when you do, you will impact people on a much bigger scale. Ironically, in this space, you might discover that money comes your way very quickly. Your job is to stay connected to the inner source of these results, rather than the results themselves. The more you let go of the idea of money, the faster it comes.

I know that when someone reads a book, they want to know what they should expect to get out of it. I realize and honor that you are choosing to spend your time reading this, so I promise to make it worth your while—however, I want to offer you the opportunity right now to completely release the need for your expectations of this book to be met. If this book met your expectations, it wouldn't be taking you beyond yourself. My goal with this book is to give you a perspective of yourself and the magic that you are in a way you've never seen before—it will never do that if your expectations of what it should be are blocking new information from coming in. Instead of creating a mental expectation of what you'll get from this book, try becoming okay with the fact that you have no idea what you might get out of it. If you don't have any expectations, then you are wide open for something completely unexpected to happen. My suggestion is this: release your expectations and open your heart. The part of you that has expectations will have a hard time understanding this book, but if you let go of the limited part of you that is trying to understand what to expect, you'll connect to something deeper that will take you into an entirely new dimension within yourself.

This book is about learning how to align with your soul. It's about removing everything from your life that doesn't support and inspire the highest you. It's about listening to those little callings that tell you things like "Leave this company!" or "Move to Italy!" and discovering that by answering these callings, you move more into alignment with your entire being and work from a higher paradigm that has faster and easier ideas for you.

This is about living fully. It's about transcending old beliefs that say things need to be a certain way. It's about receiving infinite abundant ideas and learning to act the second you feel that excited feeling. It's about making huge leaps without having all the answers and discovering that those callings are your true guidance system that has been waiting patiently for you to put your phone down and listen.

This space of possibility is waiting for us to co-create with it. It wants to move forward in a way that is much more vertical than linear. It wants to make each day exponentially better than the day before. It wants to change channels. It wants to change paradigms. It wants to destroy your old, small story. It wants to give you the world. But first, it needs you to divorce your old lifelong habitual obsession with money.

When you do, you can have it all.

# CHAPTER 2

# FIND YOUR OWN ANSWERS

This book is not about passively reading content that makes sense intellectually or that just feels good to your mind. This is about actually doing the work and shifting yourself into a place *beyond* money where you are tapping into your world-changing genius levels of creativity and value. To let go of our societal attachment to money and begin moving from a place of actual creativity and contribution, we have to completely rewire our nervous systems and separate ourselves from the lifelong habit of chasing external results. That isn't going to happen by casually reading this book while drinking tea. It's going to take the patient work of drilling into a new level of depth inside of yourself so you realize that *you have the answers* while drinking tea. The tea is not important. You can either drink tea or not. The point is, I don't want you to be dependent on this book or assume that I can do the work for you. That'd be like assuming that I could write a book describing how to work out and you could lose weight just by reading it. If that were the case, I would have already written that book and would just listen to the audio recording of it while eating burritos for breakfast. What I'm saying is, you have to actually do the work.

Do the exercises. Play full out. Allow this information to move into the cells of your body and not just get stuck in your mind. None of this will matter until it actually enters your nervous system through your actions. This book is just a starting point. This is a launchpad into you realizing that you have a million books' worth of amazing content and insights waiting to be discovered inside of you—but you still have to be the one to discover them.

I'm daring you to actually discover this part of yourself. I challenge you to transcend the illusions that have been causing you to believe that money creates your freedom, that circumstances control your happiness, or that other people's opinions of you have anything to do with who or what you are. I dare you to find your own answers. I dare you to go beyond the words in this book and connect to the wisdom you have inside of yourself that knows you are beyond all of your limiting, stressful thoughts that make you afraid of not having or being enough.

There is a mission pulling me, not to convince people to believe what I believe, but to encourage people to do the work and discover for themselves what their next step is. I want *you to connect to you.* I'm only here to offer my experiences and insights in the hopes that they might be a catalyst for you to take your next step toward uncovering more of what you already are.

An insight is something that you have *internally* (which is why it's called an "in-sight"). It's a realization that happens inside of you where your awareness goes beyond where it was before. There's nothing that I can write here that will be an insight for you—it might be an insight for me, because it came from inside of me—but for you, it's outside information. I'm only here to help inspire you to go inward and to guide you into *your own* insights that can create an actual expansion inside of yourself.

All of the things that your nervous system knows are based on experiences. All of the habits, patterns, and traits that are being held within your body and mind have come from experiences you've had that created an internal, emotional impact on you. Just reading something usually isn't enough of an experience to shift paradigms and patterns that have been held in place with years of experiential reinforcement. As you read this, I challenge you to go beyond reading. I challenge you to take what I'm saying and actually experience it for yourself. Read it in a way that allows you to feel more than think. Go beyond the mind and allow this to become an experience that shifts something real.

So, to start that process, the first thing I want to invite you to do is take a look at what you currently feel about money in your body and your nervous system. There are many different ways that money controls us that we might not notice. For instance, if you stay in a job you don't like, you're probably doing that because of money—you're declaring to yourself that money is more important than your soul's calling. Or if you have a passion that you would love to do but haven't followed it because you believe that it won't pay the bills, then that's another way that money could be influencing your decisions and overriding your heart. So ask yourself how much you're owned by money . . . are you making decisions out of a fear of losing money more than a desire to follow your passion? Do you allow money to control your emotions? Does money cause you to stay in situations that aren't fulfilling?

On a scale of 1–10, with 1 meaning you are completely owned and stressed out by money and 10 meaning you are completely free from all attachment to money and are accessing a true sense of inner abundance in each moment, how much do you feel you are currently attached to and controlled by money?

Really give yourself an honest assessment so that you can understand where you are right now. This isn't about judging yourself or feeling bad about having an attachment to money; this is bringing awareness to a way of being that almost all of us have unconsciously been trained into. Without judgment or regret, see if you can find areas that you might not have noticed where you allow yourself or your emotions to be controlled by money. Even if you feel like you're not attached to money or don't think about money that much, think about the subtle ways that money influences your emotions. Ask yourself how you feel when you lose money, like when you get a parking ticket or lose a client or job. How do you feel when you receive money, like getting a raise or an unexpected bonus? If either of those types of experiences have created any type of emotional response for you in the past, then take in that you might have some level of attachment to money.

So really give yourself a score right now, on a scale of 1–10—how much is money controlling your actions and emotions? Write it down right here if you want so you can remember it for later _____. Don't write it down there if you're reading this on an iPad or a Kindle or something; you could ruin it, which would be an expensive and strange way to start a book about abundance.

So whatever score you gave yourself, that's a representation of how much you're currently living in the illusion of money. The work we will do over the next several chapters will be about shifting that number, moving out of the illusion and into a place of being motivated much more by the calling of our soul than our mental addiction to the belief that money is in charge of us.

All of these attachments to money and external results will start to disappear when we begin to aim for something that calls to our nervous system at a higher level than money. In other words, we can't remove our attachment to money by staring at money; we have to replace money with something that is bigger and truer for us. How many times have you thought that having more money or a different circumstance or a different job would make you happy? And how many times did those circumstances change, but you were still looking for something more? We have to discover the true experience of abundance inside of ourselves instead of chasing it externally in the world—or we'll be chasing forever.

Many years ago, I had the honor of being in a couple of pretty big movies. One of them was *10 Things I Hate About You*, which came out in 1999. I remember getting the audition to play Bogey Lowenstein and being so excited, then I auditioned and started thinking, "God, if only I could get a callback," which is where you come back for another audition. Then I got a callback, and I immediately thought, "If I could only get to audition for the producers, then I'd really be something. I'd prove to myself that I'm actually talented." Then I got to audition for the producers, and I thought, "If I can just get the part, then I've really made it." I ended up getting cast for the role and shot the part, then the movie took nine months to edit, during which my main thought was "I hope my scenes don't get cut from the movie." Then the movie came out, and luckily my scenes were still in it, but by the end of the day I had already begun obsessing about if the movie was going to be a hit or not. Then it *was* a hit, and I instantly started thinking about the next role that I wanted to get.

It was almost as if the more abundance I had, the more lack I could find. While I was achieving all of these things I had dreamed of my entire life, I was making myself miserable by believing those things were going to complete me and worrying about them going away. I was so attached to the thing I was chasing that my self-worth was completely tied to it. I was moving from out to in instead of from in to out. I was letting external circumstances determine my inner state instead of discovering what I truly am and bringing that into the world.

Since then, I've discovered that there is an awareness we can move to where we understand that *we* are the source of everything we've been looking for in money or an achievement or a job or a relationship—or anything in the outside world that we believe will complete us in some way. When we're chasing something, we're not actually chasing the thing; we're chasing the experience and feeling that we think the thing will give us.

What if you discovered that you were actually the real source of those experiences and feelings you are looking for externally? Those external things are just ways you give yourself permission to experience the feelings that are *already inside of you*. This is a huge thing to understand. For instance, if you found out that you had won the lotto a few seconds ago, you'd immediately experience all of these amazing feelings of excitement and freedom and abundance. Nothing has really happened so far; no money has changed hands—you don't yet have a butler named Albert who speaks in a British accent even though he's from Fort Lauderdale— all you have is a mental excuse for why you can feel those feelings. Winning the lotto is just your excuse to allow yourself to access all of these feelings that were inside of you the entire time. If someone then told you that it was a joke and that you didn't really win the lotto, all of those feelings would immediately go away. Those feelings are possibilities that are always inside of you and are controlled completely by your perception and what you choose to believe. That means that you can allow yourself to experience all of those amazing feelings right now just by changing your perception of your situation—you don't need the external excuse.

I'm not saying to pretend you won the lotto for the rest of your life, but we will be exploring legitimate, tangible ways of how you can change your perception and raise your awareness of how abundant you actually are. So the truth is, you can feel abundant right now even if you're broke. You can feel love right now even if you're not in a relationship. The vibration of love and abundance and fulfillment exists all the time. Throughout this book, as we undo our mental attachments to external circumstances as the source of our fulfillment, those positive emotions we're looking for externally will start to show up naturally on their own because we will prove to ourselves that we are abundance, we are love, we are freedom, we are fulfillment—and the need to chase them externally will start to fall away.

Once we begin to understand that we are *the source* of what we're looking for instead of *in lack* of what we're looking for, life will begin to bring all the things we used to chase back to us as by-product. As you align with the vibration of abundance and freedom internally, life will start to mirror that vibration. This is one of the major keys to creating an abundant life. As I wrote in my first book, *I Hope I Screw This Up*, something that I've discovered for myself is that it's not "When something happens, I'll be happy." It's "When I'm happy, things will happen."

Even though our society wants us to believe that we need something outside of ourselves in order to be happy, the world is starting to wake up to the fact that we are the source of our happiness, our joy, our excitement, our creativity, our fulfillment, our freedom. We have to start moving *from* those places inside of ourselves instead of *chasing* the things in the world that we think will bring us those feelings and experiences. When you move *from* your freedom, you will create a life of freedom. When you move *from* your excitement, life is exciting. When you move *from* your joy, life becomes joyful. Nothing needs to happen outside of you for those experiences to happen inside of you. You can be in jail and still experience freedom internally. Again, this is not about tricking ourselves into feeling something that isn't real; this is about dissolving the illusion that has been causing us to believe that we're not already connected to it all.

So this book is going to help introduce your body and your nervous system to the internal experience of feeling connected to all of the freedom and abundance that you are, but it's not like flipping a switch. There's something in between you and that connection, and that's a lifetime of stagnant, fear-based beliefs that are constantly trying to save you from the fears that *it* has created. The process of moving into the experience of what you actually are can be painful at times. This is the process of true transformation. There might even be times as I write this where I will reach the edges of what I know to be true and go through pain as I let go of an old belief to make room for something bigger to show up.

There are things that you may need to let go of that are keeping you tied to your old story. There are beliefs that you might need to release. There are habits and addictions that might be supporting an old way of being that needs to die. None of those things are you. Those things are covering up what you actually are and blocking you from the incredible things you are capable of.

## Action: I Can't Hang Out Today; I Have to Change My Life and Become Incredible

*If you were working at your job in the middle of the day and a friend asked you to hang out, you'd probably say "I can't. I'm working right now. Maybe later." We often keep commitments in areas like work, but when it comes to our personal growth, we often end up sabotaging those plans and giving other things or people priority. Practice creating an intention for yourself in doing this work that is unbreakable. One way you could do this is to decide on a time each day that you are going to read this book and do the exercises—create an intention with yourself to make your growth with this book a top priority. Make your intention first. The greatest in the world make their intention and their commitment to themselves number one, and the results show up around that intention. When you do that, you'll create a consistency that will begin to build exponentially on itself and the results will be obvious.*

CHAPTER 3

# THE ILLUSION
# OF SECURITY

What did you want to be when you were a kid? An artist, a ballerina, an astronaut, Batman? Whatever it was, can you remember why you wanted to be that? I'm assuming you didn't choose that profession because you knew that firefighters get good insurance benefits or because astronauts receive high-yield 401(k) options. You probably just loved the idea of dancing or helping people or fighting crime in tights.

While some people actually end up following their childhood dream, or something close to it, many people don't—almost no one I know is Batman right now. So what the hell? Why did we all change our minds? You might think I'm about to say it has something to do with money, but I'm not. It really doesn't have anything to do with money—it only has to do with our beliefs about money.

Money, and our beliefs about money, are two *completely* different things.

We all have different beliefs about money. Some people might have learned the belief that money is the root of all evil, and as a result, are in resistance to becoming abundant. Some people may have heard from their parents that money doesn't grow on trees, which causes them to overlook opportunities where money may come easily. You might also have inherited beliefs that may seem positive about money, like that you can create freedom by having money, or that it's good to be practical, or that money creates a sense of security. Either way, if you feel like money has control over you in any way, realize that it's only your *habitual thoughts and beliefs* about money that make it seem like it has any power over you at all.

You can show this experientially to yourself right now . . . close your eyes and think about how much money you currently have (or don't have) and notice how you feel. This isn't another "on a scale of 1–10 thing"; right now, I just want you to experience all the thoughts and feelings that come up when you think about your current financial situation. Really take a moment to do this—unless you're riding a bike or driving a car or a train or a helicopter or one of those futuristic unicycle things. For all of those people, stop reading this. What you're doing is dangerous. For everyone who is stationary and responsible, take a second to close your eyes and think about your bank account, how much debt you have, all of that.

What did you feel? Excited? Fearful? Insecure? Embarrassed? Abundant? Safe?

Well, whatever you felt, realize that all I told you to do was *think* about how much money you have. I didn't say go swim in a pool of it or rub it on your body or interact with it in any real way—I said to just *think* about it. In that moment, you were only experiencing *a thought* about money. And that thought came from *you*. If you felt scared or excited or insecure, realize that all you did was experience a thought and then get scared or excited or insecure. As I like to say, this is like drawing a picture of a monster, then forgetting that you were the one who drew it and getting freaked out by it. The way you felt just now was caused by your judgment of a *thought*, not money. All of those emotions happened inside of you, not in a bank somewhere. So just open yourself up to the possibility that everything you experience around money is more about *you* than it is about money.

Your relationship to money is just a mirror of your relationship to yourself. In fact, you don't really have a relationship to money; you only have a relationship to your thoughts about money. How you feel about money is just one expression of the habitual thoughts, beliefs, and stagnant emotions that you have been carrying around in your body and nervous system for years. So if you're feeling fear around money, what you're actually feeling is a reflection of the fear and insecurity that is living inside of you all the time; you just happen to be noticing it externally through money. Money isn't causing or creating your fear; it's just bringing it to the surface.

For example, I had a friend who was in massive debt for years and was constantly stressing and in fear about money. Then that friend suddenly received a huge inheritance that allowed her to get out of debt completely and still have plenty left over. But her instant thought wasn't relief; it was *"I hope I don't lose this."* So the exact same fear existed inside of her no matter how much money she had. This is the same reason lottery winners often go broke very quickly—even though the amount of money they have has changed, they still haven't created an internal sense of abundance and worthiness to match that level of external abundance. So the same internal fear that was keeping them from being able to create money is the same fear that they are trying to cover up by buying private jets and giraffes once they finally have money in the bank.

One thing that causes us to live in this perpetual state of unconscious fear around money is the belief that *money equals security.* Money has nothing to do with security. I realize that you may hear that and think, "Yeah, but I have to pay the rent." That's true, but seeing money as your only source of security is also what is cutting you off from the infinite, creative, amazing, inventive being that you are—which would probably make paying rent a lot easier.

When we believe money is our security, we create a massive amount of stress around it. It's become this unconscious habit for many of us to live in a state of constant anxiety about our financial situation, which causes our bodies to believe they're in danger and activate our instinctual survival systems. In our attempt to create a sense of safety and security through money, we're actually creating fear within ourselves that is blocking our ability to allow new possibilities to show up.

So what is real security? It's you being fully present in this moment; it's your open heart, your acceptance of yourself, your awareness, your appreciation for life, your unconditional love—these are the real assets that make you invincible. These assets are available to you twenty-four hours a day and don't require a good credit score or approval from Chase Bank. You always have the choice to tap into your awareness, your appreciation for life, your unconditional love. That's all available to you right now, but we usually don't use all the infinite abundance that we have in this moment. The ego is constantly overlooking all the assets that are available so that it can create a reason to go chase more (I now understand why

Chase Bank is called that!). If you bring awareness to all the things you have right now, you will realize you are massively abundant. If you have total access to your open heart, your presence, and your appreciation, it really doesn't matter what is happening outside of you—you're already accessing the kind of internal security that most of the world is trying to achieve through money.

The belief that money equals security is what causes many insecure people to be completely owned by money and to do things that harm other people, the planet, and themselves. They are obsessively chasing an illusion of external security. The truth is, we can never actually be fully secure externally—we're flying through space at thousands of miles an hour in a solar system with exploding stars all around us. We live on a planet with bears. There are spiders everywhere. Even though we try to convince ourselves otherwise, we ultimately have very little control over our external security. Life is very temporary. So if there's actually no way to be completely secure externally, the only place where an experience of real security can happen is inside.

There is a space inside of you that can't be touched by anything that happens around you. This is where you have access to true security. True security is knowing that you are not your external circumstances. True security is befriending all of the insecure fears that show up in your mind. True security is falling in love with the unknown and making it your home. True security doesn't even care about spiders. If you think this transient, temporary thing called money is your source of security, you will always be insecure, even when you have it.

You will never be able to change your feeling of insecurity by having more money. Money is never the *cause* of the way you feel; it's an *effect*. Meaning, if you're broke and think that you feel unsafe because you're broke, it's probably the other way around—it's more likely that you're broke because you have a deeply held belief that you are unsafe. And it's the belief that you are unsafe that may be causing you to feel, think, and act in ways that create circumstances which mirror that belief.

Of course, you can also have lots of money and still feel unsafe—because the security is outside, not inside. This is the case for many people who have built up a motivated, high-achiever personality to try to fix a deep pain they have inside. In fact, many people who are extremely rich feel the need to have bodyguards and crazy security, which shows how that internal feeling of insecurity can still show up regardless of what the circumstances are. There are many extremely rich people on the planet who, deep down, also feel very insecure.

This brings to mind a client that I worked with recently who shared with me how he was bullied constantly as a kid. As an adult, he created a huge business that was bringing in over a million a month in profit. After working with him for a while, we discovered that bringing in massive amounts of money was his defense mechanism against being bullied, but because that childhood fear was still living inside of him, he was still totally unhappy and terrified of not being good enough. Even though the bullies were gone, he was still bullying himself by believing he's nothing without money. As soon as he started to understand this and meet himself fully by beginning to become a space of acceptance for his childhood pain, he realized that he didn't need, or even want, that much money and sold his huge house and cut his business way back. His obsessive need for money was actually blocking his ability to access a true feeling of security and safety—regardless of how much he made. In letting go of his addiction to that external validation, he transcended the old story that was keeping him stuck in his childhood fear and grew into a place of actually feeling safe and secure within himself.

Now, I know that example, on the surface, might not seem like it relates to everyone, because not everyone has millions of dollars, but ask yourself, "Am I unknowingly chasing a mind-based, external goal as a protection from something painful?"

I can tell you, from all my experience and the work I've done with people, no one's pain goes away once they reach that external goal. Oftentimes the pain gets even worse, because what they thought was the solution to the pain didn't work, so they feel hopeless on top of it all. They also may feel guilty or think, "What's wrong with me?" because they have all of these things that were supposed to make them happy. I believe that this is one of the main reasons that many celebrities and successful people end up addicted or dead. They've achieved high levels of external success with the belief that it would heal their internal wounds, but it didn't. Jim Carrey once said, "I think everybody should get rich and famous and do everything they ever dreamed of so they can see that it's not the answer."

So instead of chasing an external goal as a way to create an illusion of safety and ignoring the part of ourselves that is feeling incomplete, let's stop for a second, take a breath, and learn to give space to the thoughts and beliefs that are telling us that we need something outside of us to feel safe. Try that now. Take a deep breath and feel in your body and mind all the emotions, thoughts, or tensions that might be coming up to be seen. Allow everything to be there exactly as it is and notice that you are the awareness that it's all happening in. Become the safe space for yourself to feel everything you are feeling without judgment or fixing. Become *your own source of security.*

This is how we create actual freedom—it's not by building a huge company and having an endless amount of money; it's by finally seeing yourself fully and accepting every single part of you. A huge business and income can still show up, but if you're not connected to yourself first, you'll have no foundation and will become attached to the external, temporary thing more than to your internal source of actual abundance—and that lack of foundation will likely cause your business and finances to collapse because your business and income will almost always match what you are feeling inside. You have to find the foundation inside first.

So, before you move on to the next chapter, where we'll go deeper into the experiential process of creating actual security, take a second to let some of this sink into your body and nervous system. Feel free to read this chapter again, maybe reading more from the whole of your being and your entire body than from your mind. Many of the fear-based beliefs that you've had in your life have been there since childhood, so they're not going to immediately disappear from reading a few pages in a book—no matter how expertly those pages were written, and no matter how handsome and fit the man is who wrote them. What I'm saying is, give yourself a second to process this idea that there is an entire system of beliefs that have been cutting you off from the infinite level of abundance—which goes way beyond money—that is available to you in each moment. If a fear or doubt about that comes up, just be a space for it, and let it be there. See if you can find the place beyond the fear or doubt that can actually have love for your fears. That's the access point for the real freedom and security you've been looking for in money.

## Action: Belief Relief

Write down twenty different beliefs that you've had about money in the past. They may be beliefs that you learned from your parents or in your own experience like "Money equals freedom" or "Money equals stress" or "I'm not good with money." Whatever it is, write down twenty beliefs that you are now aware of, then notice them as they show up throughout the next few days.

# CHAPTER 4

# THE ILLUSION OF BEING BROKE

Right now, you might be saying, "So cut the shit, Cease—how do I actually get to this place of true security and safety so I can start making money?" Well, first off, realize that your mind is asking that question—and also realize that your mind is strangely violent right now for no reason, so just calm down for a second. Remember, it's only your mind that believes you are not already in a state of true security and safety. As I explained in the last chapter, the feeling of true security is not a destination that you can get to; it's something that is already inside of you. I know that the sentence "true security is inside of you" might sound kind of cliché and like something the dad from *The Brady Bunch* would say, but we're going to actually find proof of it.

If you stand under a light and close your eyes, that doesn't mean the light isn't there. You might not be able to see it, but it's still shining on you. Even if you can't feel a sense of security inside of yourself right now, that doesn't mean it's not there. You can trick yourself into believing it doesn't exist, but it will never go away. True security is constant—your beliefs are just blocking it.

There's no quick fix that I can give as a shortcut to experience actual security and freedom. I'm not saying that it will take you a long time, but I am saying that you can't trick the universe. You can't just put Post-it Notes up all over your house that say, "I AM SAFE AND SECURE" and then brainwash yourself into the experience of true, lasting internal security. That might be a good start, but if you don't go deeper, it's the same as trying to trick your mind into thinking you are secure by having millions of dollars. Trying to mentally convince yourself that you are safe with affirmations is simply creating another temporary illusion that will only feed into the addictive cycle of being controlled by your mental fears. You are already safe. You are already secure. You just might not be aware of it yet.

The reason there's no quick fix that will pull you out of the illusion of security and into a space of actual security is because it's not something that you do—it's something that naturally shows up when you stop addictively reaching for things outside of yourself to feel safe. When you stop trying to numb or fix the scared, painful emotions living inside of you, you discover that there's nothing to run from. Those fears and difficult emotions are actually the gateway to true freedom and security. They are the gateway to real creativity. They are the gateway to you. When you're fully meeting your fearful emotions, what you are experiencing is the momentary pain of your illusion dissolving. You're feeling a layer of mental stagnancy burning up in the presence of your awareness. You're in the process of moving from what you used to be into what you are about to become. You're going through labor—birthing an entire new you. Could you imagine if a mother giving birth decided that it was too difficult and went to go watch Netflix instead? That's what we're doing when we deny what we're feeling and try to fix it with something external. We're stifling our growth and choosing to allow the pain of our past to determine our future.

One example of this could be addictively overeating—if whenever emotional pain or insecurity comes up, someone were to reach for food instead of feeling their pain fully and allowing it to dissolve, they'd begin to gain weight and become unhealthy. Gaining weight and becoming unhealthy could cause them emotional pain and insecurity in many different ways, which might cause them to addictively reach for *more* food to cover that pain up again. Each time, as they stacked on more pain and insecurity, it would become more difficult for them to face their emotions, so they'd be stuck in this addictive cycle where the unresolved pain of their past is in complete control of their future—preventing them from growing into the next highest version of themselves.

There are so many feelings we have that just need to be seen. Think about all the ways that you bury your feelings and chase some other type of experience as a distraction. It's time to let ourselves experience what is really coming up. Getting out of this type of addictive cycle and finding actual security is as simple as sitting and paying attention to what's going on inside of you. When pain or fear shows up, followed by an impulse to do some addictive or distractive thing, notice that impulse and choose to be with the fear or pain instead. If you're someone who finds it hard to sit quietly with yourself, that may be a sign that you feel uncomfortable or insecure on some level and have gotten used to ignoring it. By being with yourself fully and becoming a space of acceptance for all your repressed emotions, regrets, fears, and guilt, you prove to yourself that you are bigger than all of it. You stop being *owned* by it. You stop needing to chase money or achievement or fame or status in order to overcome your internal sense of insecurity. You become secure in your surrender to your insecurity.

It's this practice of constant acceptance and emotional release that allows us to change channels and move into a new vibrational dimension. In this dimension, higher ideas and collaborative creativity allow us to bring more value into the world and create real abundance. This dimension is a real thing. There is a completely different dimension of you that is free of stagnant, unworthy stories and limitations. There's a level that your mind might hear this at, but it's not until you leap, let go of heavy things, release the results, and accept *all* of yourself that it starts to become real for you. It wasn't until I actually went through this shift that I began to understand how real this higher dimension is. There is literally an experience of seeing a completely different world, where each moment has so many more possibilities than it does problems, where inspired ideas are happening constantly, where abundance is a natural way of being. Money is a part of that abundance, but so is passion, fulfillment, connection, and contribution. When we're able to accept and transcend our fears with acceptance and love instead of obsessing over them, we connect to this higher dimension that allows us to access both *internal security* and *external abundance* at the same time.

As I mentioned, when money is our only source of security, we're not able to access all of the assets that are available to us because our minds are constantly trying to save our lives and believing that going broke means death. We immediately create strategic, short-term mental solutions when money is tight instead of allowing ourselves to expand past the fear of going broke and open up to higher-level solutions. Even when we have plenty of money, there's often a subconscious fear of going broke that is preventing us from actually feeling safe. We can't go beyond our attachment to money if we think that we're going to die if we don't have money.

I actually believe that the more you are okay with being broke, the more you become a space for this real feeling of security and abundance to show up. That might sound crazy to some, but a fear of going broke is often what is blocking us from taking the risk of bringing the full creative expression of ourselves to the world. Remember, the idea of going broke is just that—an idea, a thought, a mental concept. If you're not okay with the idea of going broke, you're at war with something inside your body that *you've* created. When you can fully accept the possibility of going broke, money stops owning you and you can start to make decisions based on your inspired ideas and callings instead of your fear.

For example, if someone is completely horrified of going broke, that person might be afraid to take chances in their career or invest in their business and end up missing the exponential growth that could have come from moving beyond their fear. J. K. Rowling was extremely poor when she wrote the Harry Potter series. Had she honored a fear of being broke, we might not have Harry Potter. Instead we might have Barry Notter, a less inspiring and more pessimistic character she came up with while working a day job she hated.

I recently had a client who was really struggling with money, and he was extremely depressed because of it. I worked with him on releasing his pain around money, then saw him again three months later . . . he actually had *less* money but felt really free and happy. Now, I realize this may seem like a terrible endorsement for me on how well I can help people become abundant, but the first step toward actual abundance for him was to be able to understand that the main cause of his pain was actually a *fear* of not having money, not the reality of not having money.

If I had just helped him create a bunch of money, it would have numbed his pain enough to gloss over an important lesson he was about to learn. Once he actually experienced the reality of what he was afraid of, he realized that he was still alive and that there was still so much to be grateful for, and he was forced to cultivate his internal source of abundance in the absence of external abundance. He now has a blank canvas and a foundation to create things out of inspiration instead of fear. I would much rather be in the position he is in now than have millions of dollars and not understand that I would also be okay if I were broke.

If you could understand and experience that you could be completely okay if you went broke, then you might create a relationship with money that isn't life and death, create a feeling of true security, and free yourself up to create on a higher level. So I have an exercise for you that will play with the idea of being okay with going broke and discovering actual internal security.

Imagine losing everything. Create the experience in your mind of literally having everything that you own taken away from you. I know that might seem depressing or scary, but like I said, going directly into our deepest fears is actually a gateway to freedom, so really think about what that would be like if you lost everything you have: your job, your savings, your car, your home, every single penny. What would that feel like?

Mentally and emotionally put yourself in that situation for a moment and feel in your body what it would be like to have absolutely *nothing* and be completely homeless, with no one to help you.

Once you're really feeling what it would be like, write down or name in your head all the emotions that you experience. Do you feel intense fear? Panic? Total vulnerability? Sadness? Hopelessness? Anger? Powerlessness?

Now, no matter what you're feeling—ask yourself this: What do you think it would take for you to still feel completely safe in the middle of all of those emotions, and with no external safety? How big of a space of acceptance would you have to become to love all the fear that might be coming up and not go into total terror? Imagine having nothing, but somehow being able to sit on a park bench and still be able to experience the beauty of nature all around you. Imagine being totally vulnerable externally, but also feeling fully present and appreciative just to be alive. How powerful would you have to become to endure all of your psychological attachment to external things being ripped out of you? To still somehow find appreciation and joy and love and compassion in that situation, *who would you have to become?*

*Huge Disclaimer:* I am not telling you to actually do this. I am not saying you should quit your job and be homeless and live on the streets. This is an exercise. *Don't* do this in real life.

If you were able to have nothing, yet somehow still experience a feeling of peace and internal security, you would probably become the most powerful person on the planet. You would have found what every single person is looking for. Remember, millionaires often go to Buddhist monks to find happiness; the opposite rarely happens.

*Smaller Disclaimer:* I am also not saying you need to be a Buddhist monk; this is just to make a point.

If you were able to have nothing yet still feel safe, you would have freed yourself from the limiting mental attachments that block you from entering true alignment with the flow of abundance. In that place of freedom and connection, I fully believe that you would be able to create on a level that you have never experienced before. You would move into a vibration of freedom and collaboration where you'd be receiving ideas of how you could share the insights you've found, help other people, or contribute in some way. Figuring out the basics of survival would be obvious to you, and you'd step into true inspiration and service and would become a massive space to receive. You would probably very quickly begin to create an *external* abundance that would match the *internal* feelings of freedom and abundance you were experiencing.

It could be very easy to hear this and think that what I'm saying is: to find this place of acceptance and freedom you need to sabotage all your current situations and make them fall apart so that you can transcend your attachment to money. That is absolutely *not* what I'm saying. I'm emphasizing this because I once had a client who decided he wanted to go to Las Vegas and put all his savings on red at a roulette table so that he could release his attachment to money. I'm not suggesting that at all—if you're going to do that, always bet on black.

Seriously though, I'm not saying to aim for the worst situation possible so that you can overcome it; however, what would happen if you had a calling in your life that was exciting and expansive and you leaped toward something that *risked* everything, in order to move beyond where you've been? That's the type of freedom that comes from being okay with going broke—the freedom to go beyond your fear and toward something greater.

So does being safe in the face of losing everything seem possible to you? If it does seem possible—and maybe even a little exciting—then that means there is a crack in the shell of your mental addiction to external circumstances and you're starting to see how security does not depend on a situation being a certain way. If it *doesn't* seem possible to you, then notice the voices that are coming up with reasons why it wouldn't be possible. Those are the voices that are working their asses off trying to hold the shell together. We'll deal with them later.

## Action: Silence Is Security

*Sit and listen for an hour to the silence that is beyond the mental desire for money or the fear of going broke. This is where your actual security is.*

# CHAPTER 5

# I LOVE MY CURRENT BANK ACCOUNT

One common denominator between pretty much everyone I've ever talked to about money is that they want to change how much they have. Most people want more money. A few want less. Some people wish money didn't exist because they hate thinking about it. But in all cases, those people are still in a fight with what their situation is in this moment and creating a war within themselves. They're saying that where they are right now isn't enough. They're telling their bodies and nervous systems that something is wrong, and in that space of conflict within themselves, they cut themselves off from a feeling of wholeness and the infinite creativity that could be coming through. If you've experienced a feeling of needing your bank account to be different, realize that you're cutting yourself off from everything you are right now by saying that this moment isn't okay and living in a fantasy that the future can be better than this . . . and let me tell you something, *there is no better moment in the future.*

There is nothing but this moment, and it's only your level of acceptance of it that can make it feel better or worse. The future is a concept that lives in our mind (like money) that cuts us off from tapping into the total abundance and joy that is available right now. The idea of later is a symptom of not accepting right now. The idea of more money is a symptom of not accepting right now. The idea of a better body, a better relationship, a better mood, and so on, is all a symptom of not completely accepting right now.

Can you be okay with right now? Can you be okay with how much money you currently have or don't have? If you feel that you don't have as much as you would like, can you find the space underneath that belief where you can still be okay with where you are right now, even though your mind is saying it's not enough? Can you sink into the feeling and inner knowing that abundance is all around you, regardless of the belief you have about what the number in your bank account says? Acceptance of where you are doesn't mean that you can't bring more money or a better body or a better relationship into your life; acceptance of where you are is what creates the internal abundance that will allow you to actually receive external abundance in a sustainable way.

So, in the old paradigm, we were told to think positively or focus only on what we want—many of us have probably made vision boards or written out goals that we want to achieve. That's amazing, and at one point that was the highest action that we knew and was actually a true expansion out of victimhood. But now we're moving to a time where there are many people who have achieved many of their goals and, as I said earlier, have discovered that achieving the things they want doesn't necessarily bring happiness. So now, this new level of awareness is coming through and we are realizing that our abundance isn't in creating something outside of us; it's in our total acceptance of every single part of ourselves. To only focus on the positive is implying that there is a negative, which makes it *impossible* to truly love all of yourself. If you're trying to think positively and only feel positive emotions, then you are running from parts of yourself and not accepting all that you are and all that you've experienced. This old paradigm is denying the perfection of this moment and the perfection of you.

I'm discovering that you can develop a level of acceptance that will allow you to see and experience everything in your life as perfect, exactly the way it is right now, and that your acceptance will create room for you to move in a completely different direction. This isn't make-believe, it's just the truth: everything is actually perfect. The universe doesn't make mistakes. You have the perfect amount of money right now to help you learn whatever lesson you need to learn. You have the perfect relationships in your life to help you discover exactly what you need to discover about yourself. None of this is random; it's a perfect synchronistic collaboration that is designed to continuously bring life to a higher level of expansion through each one of us.

This awareness moves you up in a vertical way and beyond the situations you've been trying to figure out with the limited, linear solutions your fear has been giving you. Your circumstances will begin to mirror you as you step into the perfection that you already are. By accepting the parts of you that are afraid of being broke or growing old or breaking up or falling apart—and truly loving them until they are able to leave—you will access a new ability to experience the perfection of life in ways that you've never seen before. Remember, fear cannot exist in a true space of love. If you have beliefs about yourself that you are judging, and you truly love them and accept them, they cannot exist. It's your resistance to something that creates your fear. It's not the thing you're scared of; it's your *resistance* to the thing. *That's* what's bothering you. Even the fact that you are bothered by something is part of the perfection and can be given love from a higher awareness, which will allow it to leave.

I understand that you may currently be experiencing situations that are difficult or truly sad. Something being sad or difficult to experience doesn't mean that it's not a part of the perfection of life. Even our sadness is perfect. You might notice that when you are able to accept and fully embrace your sadness, there's often a feeling of love on the other side of it. If I'm okay with my sadness, it has room to leave. When I'm judging the sadness and saying it shouldn't be there, it stays there and I never get to the love on the other side. It's because of our constant protection from the emotions our minds see as negative that we often don't get to experience the emotions that we perceive as positive. That's why I've said many times that the amount of light you emit is not based on how positively you think; it's about how much of your darkness you can accept.

When we remove all of these mental judgments about what is good and what is bad, that's when the perfection of life starts to come into our awareness. Perfection doesn't mean having the perfect circumstances; the experience of life being perfect just shows up when we're not judging it. It's the joy of pure experience. In the absence of our judgment, life will explode, in a good way. This place of full acceptance of all of ourselves and of all of life is where our true abundance comes from. Real abundance is realizing that life is perfect, exactly the way it is right now. Most of the world sees money as its source of freedom, but if you have money and are afraid of losing it, then you're actually creating a mental prison for yourself that is cutting you off from *actual* freedom. I would rather be broke and experience the true freedom of being able to see the perfection of life than be a millionaire and be closed off from it.

So what is blocking you from experiencing real abundance and being able to see the perfection of life right now? It could be a belief that you're too young or too old. It could be a belief that you're not talented enough or don't have enough experience to do what you want to do. It could be a belief that you're not worthy of feeling real abundance or love or acceptance. Whatever it is, *that* is the portal to your infinite abundance. Learning to accept an unloved part of your life, and yourself, is the gateway to being able to first experience the perfection of life internally, and then moving in a way that begins to organize your life into alignment with that perfection. You can't do it the other way around. You can't wait for life to look exactly the way your ego thinks it should *and then* learn to love it. You have to learn to enjoy and appreciate the thing you want before it ever arrives—or you'll be waiting forever.

So how do you do that? Well, like anything else, you have to practice. Appreciation is a skill. Acceptance is a skill. Surrender is a skill. Releasing judgment is a skill. Many people have goals or fantasies about making more money, but very few people have a goal of increasing their ability to appreciate life more. Imagine if you spent as much time working on your ability to appreciate and surrender as you did on your career. Imagine if you spent forty hours a week honing the ability to constantly be grateful that you're even alive at all. If a person spent as much effort tuning to the internal vibration of gratitude as they did entangling themselves in the external circumstances of their life, I truly believe that every problem they thought they had would completely dissolve.

Appreciation, surrender, releasing, accepting—these are all things that we can choose to start bringing into our lives immediately to help us undo the layers of protective stories that are causing us stress and preventing us from accessing our abundance. If you're in a situation where you think you need more money, it's your job to first accept and surrender to where you are, without any judgment or guilt about how you got there. Become a space of love for all of those painful feelings that feel like it should be different than it is: the voices that say you're not good enough, the beliefs that say it's hard to create money. As you patiently sit undistracted with all your thoughts and emotions, your old story will slowly begin to leave through your acceptance of it. And try this: for anything that is hard for you to accept, say the thing out loud and then say ". . . and I love that." So you might say something like "I'm afraid of being broke, and I love that" or "I don't think I'm enough, and I love that" or "I believe it's hard to create money, and I love that." When you bring love to whatever your beliefs are, you create a space for your judgment to leave, and when the judgment leaves, you create room for possibility.

On the other side of that judgment, you might suddenly realize and appreciate for the first time that you have a lifetime supply of oxygen all around you. You might acknowledge how your heart beats completely for free. You might notice that the sun doesn't charge you anything to shine on you and that your imagination is a magical gift beyond comprehension that was given to you for some reason you don't even understand.

We often get in the habit of appreciating only the things that we pay for. If you've ever been offered a free ticket to see a movie, you might have noticed how much less interested you were in seeing that movie. It's really true that the best things in life are free (oxygen, gravity, sunlight, love, connection, our planet, our body, meditation . . . ), but because we don't pay for them we often *miss* the best things in life. Expanding your abundance is really expanding your awareness of appreciation to include those things that we usually overlook.

To appreciate literally means to increase value; the more you appreciate yourself and the world around you, the more you raise your value and your ability to receive value. Living in the field of appreciation lifts you out of the problems that so many people are obsessed with. While one person is going crazy and screaming at people in a traffic jam, another person in the car right next to him could be in the vibration of appreciation and thinking how amazing it is that we even have cars. It's in that kind of vibration that forward-moving ideas can come to you. I once heard a story about someone who called being stuck in Los Angeles traffic their "temple" and that they often had many of their best business ideas there in the vibration of appreciation. The experience of appreciation is open and spacious and makes room for inspired creativity to come through. When you're in the problem, there's no room for solutions to show up.

Staying at the level of the problem while trying to solve it is kind of like trying to paint the walls of your house while there's a murderer in the living room. You can't paint the house until you figure out how to get the murderer to leave. And usually, murderers don't leave unless you put down the paintbrush and really make an effort. At least that's been my experience of dealing with home invasions while painting. You have to consciously accept and release whatever judgment you're holding on to about yourself or your current situation before a new level of possibility can show up. You need to give your inner murderer a hug and show it some appreciation, because the more they feel loved, the less they're going to want to murder. They might shift from being a murderer to giving you a nice, light strangle—and then eventually a deep-tissue massage.

The process of developing skills like appreciation, acceptance, and surrender is the real work, and what I hope to show you how to do in this book. Like I said, there is no quick-fix affirmation or crystal that is going to do this work for you. These are skills that require true patience and intention to develop, but when you put in the work of expanding beyond your old protective story, you start to experience the game of life in a totally different way. You begin to move exponentially. You go from trying to control the external world through manipulation and force into first becoming aware of your reactions to the external world, expanding into a space of true acceptance and surrender, and finally allowing inspired creativity to fill the space that you've made in that moment. This is how you truly move into flow. This is how you create massive abundance. This is how you change your world.

## *Exercise: Loving the Murderer*

*We all have many unconscious limiting beliefs and fears lodged inside of our body. The main reason they are still stuck there is that we haven't truly seen them and loved them. If you want to release something, you have to fully see it, hear what it says, and become a space of love for it. So write down some beliefs that you carry around that make you feel limited. Here are a few examples: I'll never amount to anything. I don't have enough time. I'm not attractive.*

*After you write down all the limiting beliefs that come to mind, go through each individual belief and allow yourself to feel love for it. Become a space outside of those beliefs that is loving them—those beliefs are not you. This might sound corny, but imagine giving your beliefs a hug, or giving them compassion the way a parent would comfort their child who was hurt. It could also help to write down "and I love that" after the beliefs. This might feel awkward at first, or you might feel like you don't yet fully love those beliefs, but the more you practice releasing resistance to the negative beliefs you have about yourself, the easier it will get to let them fall away.*

# CHAPTER 6

# RAISING YOUR VALUE

If, as you've been reading, you've discovered things about yourself that you didn't know before, have remembered something that you forgot, or have been feeling expanded or excited, then realize that you have been raising your value. By choosing to spend your time and your money on something that is helping you to deepen your connection to yourself, you are raising your value.

Many people believe that their value is based on how much money they have. They talk about what their "net worth" is and assume that everything they have accumulated is what makes them valuable, but your value is not what you have in the bank or your job or your business connections. Your true value is based on how closely connected to *yourself* you are. It's about how much access you have to the infinite nature of your being. What you are is infinite creativity and infinite value, so if you are deeply connected to yourself, then you are connected to your infinite value. You may not completely believe that you have infinite value yet—that's okay, that's why I wrote this book.

If you don't yet believe or truly feel in your body that you are infinite creativity and infinite value, do you at least believe that you have an infinite imagination? If not, then think of an elephant. Now picture a giraffe. Now think of an elephant with a giraffe's neck and the face of a lion. See—you can think of *anything*. You do have an infinite imagination. If you can think of things that don't exist, then you can bring them into the world. Some things might be harder than other things to physically bring into the world, like the lio-ephanti-raffe, but there's still an unlimited amount of possibilities. Every single invention, every piece of art, every building, every song, every book— did not exist in this world until it was created.

Even though we have these unlimited imaginations that let us create almost anything we can think of, most people don't use their imagination to create what they want—they focus on what's going wrong. They use the infinite resources of their mind to create worst-case scenarios and then spend all their creative energy trying to fix or prevent things that haven't even happened yet. This is one major cause of our anxiety. In many ways, anxiety is a sign that you are a creative genius but aren't channeling your creativity into something that inspires you. For me, anxiety mainly shows up when I'm not living in my highest creativity—it's usually when I'm doing something that I've gotten used to, my mind is bored, and I'm not being pulled into something that is taking me beyond myself. The weird thing is, people's anxiety or stress around not having enough money is using the exact same creative energy that could actually create millions—if it were channeled into this moment instead of constantly building an imagined nightmarish future that doesn't exist.

So your value is not based on how much money you have, because you are the *source* of value. You are the source of money. You are the source of creativity. You are connected to all of it. Money might fly at you the moment you start to realize the true value that you are, but money does not create what your value is. Money showing up can be a result of you stepping into the infinite value that you always have access to, but it's a *result* of your value, not what makes you valuable. It's like you have this infinite bank account in another dimension in the form of unlimited ideas and creativity, and all you have to do is transfer it into this dimension by bringing your creativity into the world. The way you develop the ability to connect with those ideas is by accepting and moving beyond all the limitations and fearful beliefs that are cutting you off from what you actually are. Those ideas will show up as soon as you stop carrying the belief that you are not worthy of them. So by reading this book right now, you're slowly undoing those habitual beliefs that keep your infinite bank account out of reach, and you are moving closer to accessing your true value.

Think of someone like Oprah. Oprah is extremely rich. But Oprah isn't just rich, she's valuable. She has tapped into an aspect of her unlimited creativity and is bringing ideas into this world in a way that makes her very valuable. If Oprah's account were wiped out tomorrow, she'd still be incredibly abundant and able to instantly create millions because of the value that she has developed through years of stepping more and more into the full expression of herself. Her open heart, her ability to talk with people and help them share their stories, her ability to connect with herself and others, her gratitude, her generosity—these are all assets she has created. By raising her value, her bank account followed.

Now imagine someone who also has hundreds of millions of dollars, but instead of learning to connect with themselves and accessing their internal value to create their money in a sustainable way, they inherited or won it somehow. If they lost everything, they might not be able to create the same type of instant value that Oprah could—they have the same *potential* to create value that Oprah does, like everyone—but they might not be aware of that potential because they haven't built the same internal awareness of value that Oprah has.

If you make money more important than your connection to yourself, you'll probably end up losing both—you won't be able to sustain external abundance if your internal value doesn't match it. If you see your bank account as worth millions but don't see *yourself* as worth millions, you will unconsciously do whatever you can to make sure the money matches what you think you are worth.

So what are the ways that you can start to actually raise *your* value instead of just your bank account's? Well, there are many different ways—moving beyond old beliefs, accepting all of yourself, harnessing your appreciation—anything you do that moves you away from the addictive patterns and limitations of your mind and closer to your connection to yourself and your natural creativity is raising your value.

We can also raise our value by simply *seeing ourselves as more valuable.* The same way we often don't allow ourselves to feel love until we have the external excuse of being in love with someone, we also don't allow ourselves to feel more valuable until we have an external reason for why we are more valuable. In other words, most of us probably wouldn't truly believe that we're worthy of making $10 million a year until we actually start bringing in

$10 million a year. Because we're so dependent on some type of external validation of what our value is, we usually see ourselves as worth only what we are currently receiving (obviously, we can receive value in many different ways, not just money). So typically, we look at what we're currently receiving and then reinforce the belief that this is what we are worth by continuing to think and take action from that limited level of value, which creates a similar level of receiving and starts the cycle all over again. But what if we were able to bypass needing an outside reason for feeling more abundant and were able to enter into a higher vibration of value directly? What if we could instantly begin to feel and act in a way that made us more valuable?

I recently watched a client of mine, Sarah, do exactly this within a matter of a few days. Sarah is an incredibly talented musician—sometimes she'll get booked to perform at big venues and open for huge bands where she'll get paid up to $10,000 a night. Even though she was already enjoying a level of success, when I worked with her, I noticed that she spoke and asked questions about her career from a place of fear, so I asked her what was in her life that was bringing her value down. I learned that for the last ten years or so, even though she was getting these major gigs and seemed to be on the verge of a huge career, she was also still performing at a bar on the weekends for $300 a night.

It was obvious to me that constantly going back to this place that valued her at a level below what she was actually worth was a major thing that was creating a lower internal value in her. She had a story around this bar that made her afraid to leave it—and it also was making her unable to receive the amazing possibilities that were right in front of her. Why would anyone pay more for her if she was constantly accepting gigs at a lower amount and telling the world that's what she's worth? It's not about going to a level where she makes more money; it's about expanding to the level where she's on the edge of her creativity, sharing her gift with more people, and doing something that is a "hell yes" in her body. Performing at the bar was like her trying to constantly install Windows 95 in her brand-new computer. It wasn't calling to her soul. In order to step into this new higher-value dimension, she needed to make space to receive on a new level by disconnecting from this thing that was keeping an old vibration alive.

So, after we discussed it for a while, she chose to make the faith-based decision to quit that job—to quit this ongoing thing that kept her just comfortable enough to not have to really grow. Once she let go of the old low-vibration job, her confidence went through the roof, the way she spoke changed, and she had a new power that was obvious when you talked to her. A week later, a booking agent that she had been wanting to work with for the last three years decided he wanted to represent her, and she was suddenly in a position to get higher-level offers all the time.

Sarah transcended her old story of what her value is by letting go of the thing she thought was keeping her safe and moving toward an excited, expansive possibility, and immediately her value went through the roof. Now Sarah only accepts gigs that are representative of this new level of value that she is embodying because she moved past the fear of risking it all and created a new internal alignment with the genius creator she actually is.

When you release yourself from the things in your life that are lowering your internal value and preventing you from growth, you'll start to naturally move toward the things that are at a higher level and increase your value even more. You might start waking up early and doing yoga instead of watching the news or scrolling through Facebook. You might start eating healthier. You'll be able to feel the things that are in support of the old story and move toward the things that support your new vibration. It could be turning off the TV and reading a book. It could be meditating more. Raising your value is about moving in a direction that is different and more expansive than what you did yesterday. It's about letting go of the things that reinforce your old small vision of what you are worth. It's doing the things that grow you and kill the old story of your limited past. It's spending your time in a way that brings you closer to yourself instead of farther away. You are the only one who can know when that is happening or what that expansive feeling is like. This is the process of learning to listen to that feeling of expansion and following it more and more.

The more you begin to honor those feelings and move toward the things that feel light in your body, the more you will begin to raise your value. Your value will start to increase because you are valuing *yourself* more. You are valuing your time more. You are spending your time doing the things that your soul is calling you toward and starting to ignore your mind's addictive pull toward old habits. Time is one of the few things that we have a truly limited supply of. The way that we spend our time is the greatest testament to how much we truly value ourselves.

If you spend your time connecting to yourself through meditation and expanding and discovering the infinite creativity that you have, then it will be very difficult to stay at a job that doesn't offer you the level of value that you know you are capable of. It will be very hard for you to stay in a relationship where the other person doesn't value you as much as you value yourself. It will be very hard for you to eat food that doesn't give a high value to your body. As you start to truly uncover the magic of what you are underneath your limiting beliefs that are telling you you're only worth a certain number of dollars an hour, your bar will begin to raise and your circumstances will start to change to match your new level of value. You raise your value by making your time more valuable. You make your time more valuable by doing only the things that expand you, change you, and move you beyond what you used to be.

If you decide that you are more valuable than watching three hours of YouTube videos about cats falling off refrigerators and instead actually change your behavior, then you will create the space for something more valuable to come through in that moment. Maybe instead of watching YouTube, you'll start writing a book, or start a YouTube channel of your own, or maybe even a new YouTube called NewTube, which will likely have an uphill battle at the start based on obvious legal issues. Basically what I'm saying is, move as if your time is temporary and money isn't—because that's the truth. You have an unlimited potential for making money and a limited amount of time on this planet. If you're spending your time as if it's infinite and you see money as something that is scarce, you're doing it backward.

You get to choose how you spend your time, and only you can determine what your time is worth. If you believe that you're a victim to what your company pays, you can give yourself an instant raise by spending your time getting to know yourself on a deeper level and bypassing all the inner barriers that have blocked you from becoming the most amazing version of yourself. If you work on yourself more than you work for other people, your value will start to skyrocket. Skills are not what is amazing. You are amazing. Someone who has a valuable skill is great, but someone who is deeply connected to herself and able to move and evolve into a higher vision every single day is priceless. It's never a lack of skills that prevents anyone from creating the income they desire—it's only a lack of connection to the calling of their soul.

I've seen people go to seminars and events where all they did was learn skill after skill after skill, but because they weren't connected to their soul, their minds were clogged up with all of these strategies, so they did nothing with them. No matter how much you teach me how to rebuild a car engine, if I'm not called to do it (and I'm not), I'll probably never be able to learn, which is why I drive an electric car—they don't have engines, I think. Anyway, if doing something is not the inspired next step in your evolution, you'll have massive resistance and difficulty in doing it. However, you can learn any skill when you're moving from the excited energy that comes from tapping into your highest calling.

Everyone on my team had very little idea of how to do many of the things that we now do in my company; we all just knew it was our calling to co-create together. As a result of following that knowing, each person on the team has blossomed into an expert in the different fields that they've expanded into. Dan had almost no experience in video editing when he started; now he's directing twenty-person film crews at our events and CGI'ing ghosts into our sketches. Kari had never produced an event before starting with me and is now a master producer of events with thousands of attendees. When we're answering our calling, all the skills we could ever need will show up. Moving from a calling is letting life do the work through you, so what you're doing becomes effortless and the results show up naturally. Money is not a calling. A job is not a calling. Tune yourself to the infinite and always-evolving calling of your soul, and the money will come.

Realize that money is completely the side effect and by-product of finding the real thing that you are looking for. What you're looking for is *you*. You're looking for your own unconditional love and acceptance. You're looking for your passion. You're looking for your creativity. Money was the side effect of Oprah moving toward her passion for hearing and sharing people's stories. Money was the side effect of Jim Carrey tapping into his childlike playfulness and completely losing himself in his artistic creativity. When you start to unlock these natural gifts inside of yourself, you will be so in love with being you that no amount of money could ever convince you to do anything other than what your heart is calling you toward. When you feel that way, that's when the money will arrive. It's a test. It's only when the money doesn't really matter that it shows up. Yes, there are people who have made money by manipulating other people, tricking other people, and hurting other people—but in doing that, those people are constantly sacrificing their connection to their soul and their joy. They will eventually feel less and less happy because they are doing things out of fear and ego, and this often makes the money they've earned unsustainable.

In this new paradigm, we find our connection to ourselves first, move from the joy of expanding into our own creativity, and bring true value to the world instead trying to trick people out of their money. In this space of self-connection, people will want to know what you have. People will want to work with you. People will be drawn to your obvious joy and will be able to trust you because you're not trying to get something from them. Think of a car salesman who isn't trying to sell you a car but is so connected to himself and internally secure that he brings you actual value and wants what's best for you—even if it means losing the sale. You would be much more likely to buy a car from him because you don't feel manipulated or pressured.

There is a whole new group of people out there who can see through BS and want to connect with people who are authentically connected to themselves and this moment. The number-one thing that you have to offer people is your connection to the moment. Even though you might be selling other products or services, your connection to the moment, your connection to you, your connection to the infinite truth of what you are—that's what people are truly wanting.

Mr. Rogers is priceless. He's worth so much more than money. He brought something timeless to the world, and he did it by being compassionate, patient, and loving. He did it by connecting to himself and bringing an incredible amount of presence to every moment, and to every person and child he interacted with. I recently learned that he meditated for two hours every morning. That practiced connection to himself and the moment is what we all connected to. We all have this foundation-based, real possibility of creating infinite value inside of ourselves. We all have the exact same potential as Mr. Rogers or Michael Jordan or Oprah . . . and our job is to make our value priceless. Our job is to become worth more than money. Our job is to connect and find a value, a presence, and a contribution to the world that is *beyond* money. When you go beyond money and create an unattached connection to yourself and the moment, you step into an unlimited flow of abundance.

The "flow of abundance" is not just something that sounds nice—*it's a real thing.* It's beating your heart, it's growing your hair, it's shining the sun, it's growing the plants. It's a creative energy that wants to move into this world in a powerful way. If you are not stepping into what you are and letting this energy flow in, then you're blocking it. You're an obstacle to life. It wants to move through you, but if your stagnant mental beliefs are standing in its way, then you're at war with that flow. That's why you feel stressed. That's why you worry. That's why you trick yourself into believing that you're not good enough or that you're not smart enough or that you're not creative enough. All of that is bullshit. It's a lie that was inserted into your brain by a world around you that has lost its connection to that abundant, loving flow. That world needs you so badly. That world needs you to free it from its lack of flow, from its blocks and limitations, from its illusion. That world needs you to actually live and be an example of the abundant flow that brings forward moving ideas and new revelations into existence.

Not long ago I got to see firsthand, in a very obvious way, someone who blocked that abundant flow from coming into their life because of their patterns of limitation and lack.

I recently felt a calling to really learn how to play piano well, so I got excited about making a commitment to take piano lessons every day for six months. I googled piano teachers in my area and called the first one who popped up. We talked for a minute, and I told him who I was, and he got all excited because he knew me and my work, and was starting to get into working on himself in this way. He was inspired and saw this as a huge synchronicity as he was looking for new clients and also wanting to change his life—so this was an amazing opportunity. So far, so good.

Two days later, he came over to the house—in a much different mood. He seemed kind of irritated and was complaining about how hard his life is and for some reason started telling me about all these people who owe him money. I offered him a few perspectives on things that I could see around some of the issues he was having, but he wasn't interested in hearing it. The vibration was feeling so off that I was starting to feel hesitant about working with him, but I had agreed to do at least one lesson, so we started anyway, and he asked me about what my goals were in learning piano. I showed him some of the music that I'd like to play, and he told me that it sucked and that I wouldn't be able to play like that any time soon. Even though I know everything is perfect and meant to be, this wasn't a great lesson.

So we finished the lesson and he left, and I paid him for the lesson via PayPal. Shortly after that, I got an angry message from him that he was upset about a $2.50 fee that he had to pay to PayPal to receive that money. As he complained to me about the fee, what he couldn't see, or remember, was that I had told him I was prepared to hire him for lessons *every day* for the next six months. I was about to write him a check for thousands of dollars for over a hundred lessons. After what I experienced in that first lesson, I realized it probably didn't align for us to work together long-term. It was fascinating to me how he was telling me about all his money problems and focusing on the $2.50 fee, while completely overlooking this huge amount of money that could have come from being present with the moment he was in. Money was trying to come to him, and all he had to do was receive it.

This whole thing was kind of shocking to me, but it made me think of how many places in my life I'm missing opportunities that are right in front of me and blocked by my limited awareness. Ask yourself: How many times have you not been able to receive what life is trying to give you because you're caught up in a story of lack? Can you think of a time where life was trying to give you peace, but you chose to argue with a loved one? Or can you remember a time where your creativity could have been flowing through you, but you were busy stressing about the guy who cut you off earlier? Or maybe a time where you could have called and connected with someone you haven't spoken to for a while, but you were too caught up with what your ex was doing? And what's trying to happen right now? What peace or possibility or creativity or forgiveness is trying to come through right this second? Are you willing to receive it, or are you focused on a problem that might not exist if you stopped focusing on it?

This flow of abundance is waiting to lift each one of us into a new level of freedom as soon as we release these unconscious limitations that keep us anchored to our problems, but we first have to actually change our value by doing real internal work. This isn't you changing you so that you can be a space that receives more abundance—this is you changing you so that you can reflect to others more of what they truly are so we can stop competing with one another and all feel the connected flow of energy that we actually are. People would never argue over petty things, hurt, manipulate, or screw anyone else over if they could actually feel the abundant flow that they are. This ability to give something that is in true service is where you become unbelievably valuable and bring something to the world that it truly needs.

## Exercise: Raise Your Value Right Now

*Learn to teach piano really well and then give me a call. I still need a teacher. Also, sit for a while in the vibration of you being worth a massive amount of money. I would really recommend an hour, but I'll leave exactly how long up to you. Know that the longer you go, the more effective this will be, so just choose the amount of time based on how much you want to raise your value. So for however long you feel, just sit, breathe deeply, and envision what it would feel like, and who you would have to become, to be worth a lot of money (the amount I'll leave up to you, too, but create an amount that is exciting and way beyond what you see yourself as worth currently).*

*Don't look for how you might be able to create that amount of money; instead, experience what it would feel like in your body to have complete real-life evidence that you are worth that much. Dismiss the how and just feel. I'm also not saying to imagine what it would be like to have millions of dollars or to picture what house you would live in or what car you would drive, only to ask yourself what it would feel like to be receiving on that level. You might discover at first that it would feel exciting, and then eventually it might become a calm, normal feeling—that's what we're looking for, for it to be normal for you to be worth a huge amount. This is the place where you begin to think, act, and move like someone who is bringing massive value to the world— and that's when the evidence of your new value starts to show up all around you.*

# CHAPTER 7

# THE HELENS

At this point, you might be saying to yourself, "Cut the shit, Cease. I need some practical real-world examples." You really don't need to be that aggressive; this is a nice book. But, you're in luck . . . in this chapter I'm going to give you a real-world example of how raising your internal value can change both your internal and external results. It's not actually a real-world example, because it's just going to be me creating an imaginary scenario in this book, but it's still going to be helpful.

Let's imagine three people. Let's call them Helen #1, Helen #2, and Helen #3 . . . that's stupid and confusing . . . let's call them Helen A, Helen B, and Helen C.

Now imagine that we give each Helen $1 million. And let's also imagine that each Helen is starting at around the same place financially. They have similar skills, are a similar age, and other than a few philosophical differences that we'll discover later, are similarly capable—maybe that's why they're all named Helen.

So Helen A gets her million dollars and is pretty pumped, as you can imagine. She immediately quits her job and rents a huge luxury apartment so she can throw parties all the time. She gets a new convertible, a new wardrobe, a giant Kid Rock statue, and a bunch of new jewelry. At the end of year one, Helen A has had some short-term fun but hasn't evolved much. Also, she has spent about half of her money already (the average Kid Rock statue goes for around $250,000, depending on your provider).

Helen B, on the other hand, has learned some basic investing principles and has been to numerous free financial seminars at her local Courtyard by Marriott Hotel. She's pretty smart with her money off the bat. She doesn't quit her job and, other than paying off some debt and making a few smart purchases, invests her money for the future. Let's say she puts almost all her money into a secure investment that will guarantee a 10 percent return, which is awesome. Pretty smart, right? At the end of year one, Helen B still has slightly more money than she started with, a new sense of security, and a long-term plan. Like Helen A, she hasn't expanded much, even though her money has.

Now let's look at Helen C. Helen C has read this book, knows that I can deadlift close to 400 lbs., and understands that her connection to herself is her number-one asset. She decides to use her million dollars only in ways that expand her. Realizing that her job is not truly her passion, Helen C actually does quit her job, just like Helen A. However, instead of throwing parties and buying overpriced statues of celebrities from the '90s, Helen C uses her free time to learn more about herself. She takes a backpacking trip around Europe because it's always been a dream of hers. She learns so many things about herself and the world that, when she returns, she feels like an entirely new person.

Feeling a new sense of freedom, Helen C now starts using her time to meditate and do yoga and get her body in shape. She hires a personal trainer and nutritionist and is feeling healthier than ever. As she feels better and better, she starts to have more energy. She is feeling excited and inspired in so many different areas of her creativity. She starts taking painting classes and dance lessons and continues traveling to new places. She decides to start a business that brings together all of her real passions. Because it feels inspired, she uses her money to invest in starting a podcast and a YouTube channel to share all the gifts and messages that are showing up for her. She also invests money in hiring people to do the work in the business that is not her highest excitement so that she can spend time expanding toward the things that do excite her. At the end of year one, Helen C has spent and invested almost half of her money but is building a business that *feeds her soul* and is feeling more alive than ever before.

So, from what you know about the Helens, who's going to win? I'm joking. There are no winners or losers here; we're all on our own journeys. What I mean is, who is the best? I'm being sarcastic. What I'm saying is, who is a much better person than the other two idiots?

Seriously though, at the end of year one, you can see that Helen A has made some short-term decisions that will probably leave her completely broke in a few short years. Even though that's extremely easy to see here, that's still the way that many of us live. We often choose the short-term egoic pleasure of television or fast food or alcohol—or whatever it is we turn to for momentary comfort—but somehow we can't see how much that is costing us in the long run. It's not just costing us money; it's costing us our connection to ourselves and the ability to discover what gifts we might truly be able to bring to the world.

So Helen A is pretty obviously going down a road that is probably going to cause her some pain in the future, but no problem—she's a great lady; I'm sure she'll bounce back.

Helen B, on the other hand, has done something that most people would say is extremely responsible, disciplined, and long-term focused. She's planning for her future and creating financial security—and that's great. When you start to compare Helen B and Helen C though, it's not so obvious who's on a path toward true abundance. Helen C has less money than Helen B at the end of the first year, and less of a concrete plan, but is starting to tap into something that is more fulfilling, soul expanding, and possibly quite a bit more valuable than the 10 percent that Helen B is getting back. Helen B is making her money secure, but Helen C is *changing as a human being.*

Helen C is moving in a way that I've found pays for itself over and over again—*investing in yourself.* This is the way that my company has basically doubled in reach, impact, and income every year for the last five years. Following my excited passion and investing in my creativity is getting much bigger results—not only in terms of fulfillment, but in literal dollars and cents—than I could ever get from a bank or the stock markets or from buying duplexes (or even just normal plexes). Instead of being a safety blanket, my money is the fuel for my creativity, and I use it as a tool that propels me into a higher level of value. Every time I take a leap and stretch myself by doing something like writing a check for a huge down payment on a theater rental or producing something, I force myself to shift into a new channel of thinking and discover higher solutions— because I've created something that is calling me in a bigger way. When I invest in my creativity, it leverages me into more of myself. It moves me forward. It moves this message forward. It fulfills my soul and moves me deeper into alignment with something so much more secure than guaranteed interest.

Let me ask you this—which one of the Helens would be doing the best if the money system somehow collapsed and all the numbers in the bank were suddenly zeroed out? We can all see that Helen A is screwed . . . and Helen B would be back to square one . . . but Helen C would still have something. She'd have her experience. She'd have her growth. She'd have her new health. She'd have a new connection and insight into herself that would probably be able to bring a new level of value even in the chaos of the world going berserk without money.

As Helen C does the inner work, she starts to create a new confidence and self-connection—what she's doing is entering the process of raising her vibration. I know that using the word *vibration* makes me sound like a hippie, but that's really the best word I can find to describe what is happening. I won't try to explain the science of it here, mostly because I don't know it, but I've had a very obvious experience in my life of moving gradually from what feels like a lower vibration, where I've felt stuck in the circumstances in my life, into a higher vibration that is filled with freedom and possibility. I've discovered that the most valuable people, and the people that I'm drawn to work with, are the people who are living in a higher vibration that feels effortless to be around.

Your vibration isn't measured by how much education you have or how much experience you have; it has to do with how connected you are with yourself. People on a high vibration see their value as higher; they're less codependent on you; they don't pull you into a lower vibration as you try to pull them up; they have an inner guidance system, and the universe is flowing through them in a powerful way. This vibration is where your value is. As you invest more in the things that raise your vibration and bring you into this higher level of alignment, that money gets to move into universal circulation, and you become an obvious safe space for life to continue sending abundance your way. This planet is evolving into a higher vibration of love, generosity, compassion, contribution—the more you get in sync with that vibration, the more life will see you as a collaborator in its evolution and give you the resources you need to make as big of an impact as you are willing to make.

So I know that in this example, all of these people got a million dollars, which you might not have, but with the money that you do have, or are about to have, what are the things that you are investing in? Are they Helen A things that feel good for a little bit and then end up costing you in the long run? Doritos, social media, lattes, magazines, cigarettes, video games, beer, fancy cars—these are all the types of things that often seem like they're a good idea in the moment and what we think we want, but years down the line end up costing so much more than we paid for them and don't bring us any closer to ourselves. Many of the things that we invest in addictively not only cause us to disconnect from ourselves and not grow, but they also have all these hidden costs because they rot your teeth, hurt your body, need to be insured, and so on. And if you have no money, what are you doing with your time? We all have the same amount of time. Are you spending your time in a way that changes you and makes you more valuable, or spending it doing something that numbs you? Are you Helen A'ing your time?

Or maybe you're investing in Helen B things that help you feel more externally secure but don't expand you.

Remember, no matter how much external security you create, you can never create true freedom unless you also create internal security, which takes expanding, growing, and moving beyond the shell of your old story. Often those external investments can become addictions that start to *own you* because you think they are your only source of security.

Many Helen C things—like meditation, exercise, nature, healthy food, traveling, classes, starting a new business—are things that might also have a cost (though many don't) but end up paying for themselves over and over in the long run in so many different ways. These are the things that expand you—they take you higher than yourself and help you step into what you actually are. These are the things that create true value. These are the ways that you prove how much you value yourself and how you declare to the universe that you deserve the abundance it has to offer.

Some people might be thinking that not doing some of the Helen A things we're talking about here would take all the fun and pleasure out of life, but ask yourself, what type of pleasure are you actually getting from those things? In my experience, it's usually a quick high followed by a low because you're looking to an external thing for happiness, and when it's over, you need another thing to take its place. Some of the Helen C things might not give as much of an instant rush but reward you with a long-term, sustainable type of joy that builds on itself day after day. This is about moving from the quick-fix, distraction-type things into the long-term, foundation-based joy that comes from honoring yourself and your true value in the things you choose to do.

When you spend all your money on addictive distractions, you don't grow and you ruin your teeth. When you keep all your money in a bank, it grows a little bit each year, gives you the illusion of security, and your teeth stay the same. When you invest your money in yourself and discovering what you actually are, you are investing in universal expansion, a perfect smile, and the evolution of your soul—which, as you can imagine, gives a slightly better return than the stock market (which is often crashing anyway).

Remember, when you invest in the stock market and real estate, that can be great, but you're investing in what other people do. There are aspects of the stock market that you have no control over. If you're doing this work, your innovation and your creativity will always be going up, and if you move like Helen C, you are investing in something that is growing exponentially. There is no potential crash if you are investing in you and truly spending your time and money in ways that expand you. Sure, you might have a project that doesn't go the way you planned, but if you are trusting your own guidance and evolution, you'll discover something in every seeming failure that actually takes you to a higher level.

In fact, one big leap that I took early on with my company was renting a big 1,400-person theater, even though we had only done 200-person events up until then. We had an original intention to do the event and also offer the audience the opportunity to work with me in small groups at weeklong retreats. Halfway through the event, I had a strong intuition that we shouldn't offer those retreats because it would keep us tied to working with only a few people at a time, so we didn't, and ended up losing a decent amount of money on that event. That might have looked like a failure from the outside, but I instantly knew it was showing us something bigger than we had seen before and opening up a new opportunity.

In the next week, with the free time we had now because we weren't planning all of these retreats, my team and I had an inspired idea to release a few different videos on Facebook, and one of them went crazy viral and got something like 50 million views. It filled our next two events almost immediately and took us to an entirely new level of impact. Because the money for that initial event was put into growth for my team and me instead of the stock market, what initially seemed like a loss has probably come back at least a hundred times by now.

So instead of investing your time and money in things outside of you, start looking at ways you can begin investing in your internal growth. Start moving toward the things that stretch you and bring you to a higher vibration. Start to notice the difference between how you feel doing Helen A things vs. Helen B things vs. Helen C things. See what happens for just one day when you move with the intention of fueling your internal growth more than your addictive need for an imaginary sense of external security—it might change everything.

## Exercise: What the Helen Have You Been Doing?

*It's time for you to do an exercise that will force you to be very honest with yourself. If you really want to find out where you've been spending your time and money, pull up your credit card and look through the last month's expenses. Go through every purchase you've made and mark down if it's a Helen A, a Helen B, or a Helen C purchase. As a reminder, if it was a Helen A expense, it was something you bought so you could entertain and numb yourself from something inside of you and didn't contribute to your long-term growth, or maybe even took away from it. If it was a*

*Helen B thing, maybe it was an investment in a 401(k) or putting a little extra into your mortgage or something like that. If it was a Helen C thing, it was something that is a long-term investment in your growth like eating healthy, taking an exciting class, going to a workshop, or delegating something that frees you up to bring a higher value to the world. As you go through your credit card statement and categorize everything as either A money, B money, or C money, you'll bring a new awareness to where you've been putting your energy in the past and open up an amazing opportunity for you to change your habits. I realize this might not be your favorite exercise—because, normally, looking through your credit card statement is not the most exciting thing—but trust me, this will bring in a new level of understanding and clarity to how you can begin to use your money and time as a powerful tool for your expansion.*

# CHAPTER 8

# 10s

One of the biggest things that will shift how you spend your time and money and move you into a higher value is starting to connect more to the guidance of your body. When I say body, what I'm really talking about is the part of you that is intuitive and connected to the whole of what you are—versus just your mind. You could also call this your higher self or a million other names, but I say *body* because, when I'm in a high vibration, I feel my awareness move from just being in my head into my entire body, and even the space around my body, in a way. This space of awareness that is beyond our mental habits is always moving us toward our expansion and seeing a perspective beyond short-term gain. When we're moving from this deeper place, we automatically make decisions, spend our money, and use our time doing things that will grow us and bring us closer to our natural creativity and value. Tapping into this deeper awareness within is where real abundance comes from.

The only problem is, we live in a world that has driven us into our heads and has disconnected us from our bodies and the full awareness of what we are. This is the only way companies can sell us stuff we don't need.

Most marketing is designed to make you feel like you won't be enough if you don't buy whatever product it is they're pitching you, which can often cause you to feel disconnected from yourself. As a result, many of us are used to buying Shake Weights, Snuggies, and other things we don't actually need—and we're spending our time in ways that stifle our creativity instead of inspiring it. If you're internally arguing with me right now that Snuggies are great, just realize that all they are is a backward robe. You don't need a backward robe. You almost don't even need a robe—just dry off and put some pants on already.

My point is, many of the things we're doing out of habit are just things that we learned to do in our past from a disconnected place. For example, if I think about something like eating a bunch of burritos, I can feel how that sounds like a good idea in my mind and that I would be able to get a feeling of instant love by doing that. I can also feel in my body how that's just an addictive high from the past that my mind is chasing and that it wouldn't be long-term fulfilling. If I think about something like meditating though, I can tell that it feels like death to my mind but expansion to my body. There's no guarantee about what I'll get from meditating; there's just a subtle feeling that is pulling me toward results that are beyond what I can see with my mind. My mind can easily see the instant high it would get from eating burritos because that is part of my old story—it knows what will happen if I do that because I've done that thousands of times. I've eaten thousands of burritos, and strangely, it's never ended all that great, but for some reason my mind still wants that predictable, instant, short-lived result of eating a delicious burrito. My mind can't see what all the results of meditation might be because the possible results that could come from it are *beyond* my old story and completely unknown.

We can't create a future that is more abundant, more free, or more fulfilling if we keep repeating all the same habits that we've learned from our past. This is where a lot of the real work comes in. We often have to experience the momentary feelings of pain that can come from breaking out of our habitual patterns and into something new. It's like driving on a paved road your entire life and then realizing that road doesn't take you where you want to go, so you have to pull off on to the dirt. In the moment, it seems easier and more comfortable to stay on the paved road, but you'll never get where you're trying to go if you do.

So instead of vaguely trying to decide if something is expansive or contracting, let's actually break it down and rate how excited in your body you would be about a few different activities. Let's use the 1–10 scale. I know there are scales other than the 1–10 scale, but I've tested it, and this one is the best for this exercise. The two-thumbs-up scale was a disaster. An absolute disaster. The 4- and 5-star systems were too time-consuming and confusing. The mustache scale didn't make sense because it doesn't exist. This is the best system, trust me.

Remember, the point of this is to feel what's exciting from the perspective of the whole of your being, beyond your old story. What we're looking for is which of these activities would take you higher than where you've been and into a new dimension of growth that feels exciting, and maybe even a little scary. Look for the difference between what is exciting to your body because it's expansive, and what is exciting to your mind because it's a habit. Drinking alcohol might be exciting to some people's mind because it's a habit, but it probably wouldn't be truly exciting to their body.

From ages twelve to around thirty-four, I was a stand-up comedian. I've performed in comedy clubs for most of my life—and have gotten a lot of love there. For me, going into a comedy club would be fun and effortless and give me a high, but it wouldn't be expansive. It doesn't take me beyond me anymore. It served its purpose. There are many reasons that I could justify why I should perform at a comedy club—the love and attention I'd get, the fun, the instant money—but I would be in conflict with the long-term evolution that my guidance system is pulling me toward.

One thing I've discovered is that if you're justifying or explaining *why* you're doing something, it's not a 10. The things in my life that I truly want to have and do, I never have to justify. I don't justify what it is that I do for a living or why I have a family; I instantly know they are a 10. If I said, "My fiancée, Christy, is not that great, but at least she has good medical insurance," then that would mean I probably don't really want to be with Christy. Luckily I do want to be with her without any justification at all and she just happens to have good medical insurance as a bonus. I'm just kidding; she doesn't have good insurance at all.

We justify so many things in our lives that we don't even notice. We justify why it's okay for people to treat us like crap by saying things like "I know they don't mean it." We justify why we live in a place we don't like by saying things like "But it's right next door to a Chipotle." We usually justify things because we're ignoring what our body is actually feeling about them. You might notice that an unfulfilling job feels like a 1 in your body, but your habitual story is afraid of losing money, so you might mentally justify why you want to keep it. This exercise is about listening to your body and dropping those justifications that your mind loves to make.

So, with 1 being the least exciting to your body and 10 being the most exciting, go through this list of hypothetical activities one by one and, without considering the cost or any other details, feel in your body how excited you would be to do them and write down a number between 1 and 10 next to it.

Work out with a personal trainer ___

Sleep in late ___

Get up at sunrise ___

Paint ___

Go to work ___

Clean the house ___

Hire housecleaners ___

Meditate for an hour ___

Eat healthy ___

Watch Netflix ___

Take a hike ___

Eat burritos ___

Buy new clothes ___

Throw out unused clothes ___

Meet new people ___

Go skydiving ___

Spend time on Facebook ___

Write a book ___

Travel to a foreign country ___

Drink alcohol ___

Eat chocolate ___

Go swimming ___

Go to dinner with your best friend ___

Buy a new car ___

Donate $1,000 to a charity ___

Learn to moonwalk ___

Go on a juice fast ___

Start smoking, or continue smoking ___

Learn a new language ___

Start a new business ___

Clean out your refrigerator ___

Drink coffee ___

Do yoga ___

Drink more water ___

Live in nature ___

Learn to play a new instrument ___

Eat potato chips ___

Go running ___

Start a YouTube channel ___

Plant a garden ___

Drive in traffic ___

Call an old friend ___

Take a class at a community college ___

Try a new hairstyle ___

Skim through this list, then decide to actually do this exercise fully ___

Okay, great. So like I said, there are no right answers here. This is just an exercise to help you start listening to the part of you that is calling you to go beyond what you used to be. We're going to be going even deeper into this in the next chapter, but just take a moment and ask yourself if there was anything on the list where you felt a mental excitement, but you knew in your body it wasn't where you would get your highest expansion? If so, *that's an amazing thing to notice.* Learning the difference between those two feelings is one major way that we truly begin to raise our value and move into actual abundance.

When more and more of the things we are doing come from an expansive calling instead of our habitual addictions, we naturally find ourselves in situations that match the expansion. If we move toward the old habits of the mind, our circumstances will start to shrink. If you want more abundance, more freedom, more joy, more contribution, and more fulfillment, you have to let go of the things that are taking up space in your life and causing you to hold on to your old limited way of being. You have to remove the things blocking your connection and your creativity. You have to step into the unknown.

---

### Action: Make Abraham Lincoln Proud

*If you didn't do the exercise in this chapter, this is a reminder and an opportunity for you to go back and do it. Just so you know, Abraham Lincoln always did the exercises that the books he read suggested that he do. That's why he ended up with such an awesome beard.*

---

# CHAPTER 9

# YOUR AVERAGE AMOUNT OF ALIGNMENT

So in the last chapter, you rated a bunch of *theoretical* things that you could be doing. In this chapter we're going to take an honest look at all the things that you've *actually* been doing recently and rate them too. This is important. It's a real-time inventory of how much you are growing into what you actually are. Think of it as another way to judge someone's net worth. What if, when you applied for a home loan, the bank didn't just look at how much money you have in the bank and your income, but also took into account how much you are living in alignment with the calling of your soul? What if your credit score was boosted by the number of 10s you're taking action on? I'm not sure how they'd officially calculate any of that, so it probably won't happen soon, but it is fun to think about for a second.

Remember, a 10 is something that aligns you more with what you truly are. Everything else is just keeping your old story alive. The universe is at a 10 constantly. It's the definition of a 10. It's creating and expanding and moving into the next highest version of itself in every single moment. Many people in this world feel disconnected and depressed, and that's because they're out of congruence with the expansion of the universe. They're not allowing the flow of life to clean out all the stagnant past that they are holding on to by constantly growing and evolving. Moving toward a 10 forces you to meet yourself as you release the old story of everything you're not. 10s are really, really powerful. They're vibration; they're a feeling; they're possibility. 10s are waking you up. When you're living in a 10, you're creating a massive space for the universe to co-create with you in each moment. 10s are your gold; they're your currency. Don't look for money anymore. Look for 10s.

A 10 puts you into unknown territory. When you take a leap into a 10, you don't know what the hell is going to happen. A 10 is not something that you can strategically plan out and understand what you're going to get from it. It's not an investment strategy. It's not something that you can manipulate so that it turns out the way you want it. Doing something that is a 10 requires you to surrender to the endless possibilities that are on the other side.

Many people are wanting to live their purpose, but instead of answering the unknown calling in their body, they want to analyze and plan and make sure that following that calling will work out the way they want. They're looking for a guarantee. That's not following a purpose. That's not moving toward a 10. That's turning a 10 into a 2 by just dipping their toe in and not fully trusting what life is trying to show them. That's bringing all their past into the moment and allowing their old patterns to block them from all the possibilities their 10 is trying to show them.

If you're holding a bunch of metaphorical suitcases that are filled with your old story and are spending your time doing a bunch of 2- and 3-type activities, then the universe can't fully create and express through you. You're blocking it with these old things that aren't a part of what is trying to emerge. It's like the universe is handing you stacks of cash, but you're saying, "Sorry, my hands are full with all of these suitcases." Inside of those suitcases is everything you *think* you need to make money, get approval, and be enough. All of that is actually blocking what you're looking for. We've got to make space for something new to come in. The same way you have to physically open your hands and let go of a suitcase in order to pick up something else, you also have to literally let go of your limited story from your past in order to let a new, bigger possibility show up.

By letting go, I mean, just stop holding on. Everything you are letting go of is not a part of you anyway. This is why sitting in silence for a while can help bring light to all the things that you thought you were and then remove them. When you are obsessed with chasing something externally or distracting yourself, you don't realize that you've been holding on to all of this nonsense that isn't who you are. When you bring a higher awareness in, you'll start to see all the false fixing, protective, chasing parts of you that have been running the show. You'll start to see how much of what you are doing in your life is motivated by a fearful story.

So what I'm suggesting you do now is use a separate piece of paper, or your phone or laptop, and make a list of basically everything that you do and have in your life. All of your habits, routines, your jobs, your relationships, any addictions, all the people you spend time with, the things you spend your money on, the things that you listen to or read, the things that you do for fun. Everything. You don't need to stress about every single tiny detail; just write down everything that comes to mind in the next five minutes or so. You also don't have to rate anything yet; first, write down everything you can think of. This is an exercise that I want to really encourage you to do, even if you didn't do the last one. *The value that you get out of this book is not just based on what you paid for it; it's based on what you do with it.* If there's something inside of you that is feeling like you don't want to do this exercise, maybe it's worth taking a look at that. Maybe that's the fearful part of your mind already making you feel pain so that it can protect itself from the growth that is about to happen. Maybe you've already started this exercise and you don't even know it. Maybe you've already discovered a habit that has been blocking you from your 10s.

Okay, so do this exercise, and I'll see you in five minutes. I'm gonna grab a snack real quick (the snack I'm grabbing is a 10).

Okay, so you've done the first part of the exercise. Now, just like in the exercise in the last chapter, go through everything and listen to what your body is telling you about it. If it's a 10, you'll know it right away. You'll be excited and feel light and maybe a little scared too. If you have to think about what number something is, then it's not a 10. The second you have to think about it, your mind is taking over and making up for the lack of excitement in your body. You'll probably also know the 1s and 2s right away. Everything in the middle, you might have to feel into a little bit, and obviously this isn't science-level accurate, so put a number that feels right without bringing your mind into it too much. Don't bring your mind into it at all, actually. Your mind will want to justify why you have something in your life: "But it pays the bills," "But I've eaten this kind of food since I was a kid," "But we had fun at that one concert that one time." Don't let those logical reasons override the feeling in your body. I know that this might feel repetitive, but this is one of the most important parts of this entire book, and I want you to really bring this into your nervous system. This is how I move, this is how the people on my team move, and it's changed our lives dramatically. It's learning how to follow your body's intuition over your mind's security and limited logic. That's what we've been doing our entire lives.

The feeling of a 10 in your body is a preview of more 10s that will show up in your life when you follow that feeling. The feeling of a 2 in your body is a preview of more 2s that will show up if you listen to the outdated logic of your old story and hold on to it. So for now at least—you don't have to take any action—just write down the honest, instinctual number that you feel in your body as you go through your list.

I'm going to grab another snack (this snack is an 8, but I got two of them, so it's a 16).

Okay, so now you've basically got an inventory of your life and how aligned you are with yourself. Now, add up all the numbers and divide *that* number by the number of things you wrote down—that's your Average Amount of Alignment. It's your AAA score.

Here's an example of what the math might look like for an imaginary person named Gerlitch:

| | |
|---|---|
| Traveling | 9 |
| My current job | 6 |
| Going drinking with Jilron and Kimborng on Fridays | 6 |
| Drinking organic green juice each morning | 9 |
| Eating fast food 3 times a week | 3 |
| Painting | 10 |
| Learning a new language | 8 |
| Scrolling through Facebook | 4 |
| Running in the woods | 9 |
| Volunteering at the homeless shelter | 10 |
| Total | 74 |

So if Gerlitch added up all the numbers he wrote down for each item on his list, he'd have a total of 74. Now if he divides that number by how many items he had, which is 10 in this case (you'll probably have a lot more), he'd have a AAA score of 7.4. Nice job, Gerlitch. I bet if you drop that fast food and Facebook, you'd be looking at a solid 8 in no time.

Your AAA score is a snapshot of what you see your value as and how much you are staying in the shell of an old story. This is your average amount of alignment with the truth of what you are. If you are constantly doing things that feel like 2s and 3s, then you are constantly doing things that are in conflict with the guidance and evolution of your soul. If you are mostly doing 9s and 10s, then you are allowing the guidance of your soul to move you toward the highest version of yourself on a regular basis, which means you are going to skyrocket. The only reason that you ever do something that you know isn't a 10 in your body is because your mind is giving you a reason for doing it that is based in the past. To *continuously* be stepping into 10s in your life, you have to *continuously* be letting go of mental justifications and going toward a vibration that feels good but doesn't have any guarantees from your past that the mind can hold on to.

Whatever your AAA score is, it's very possible that you've been living at that level of alignment for a while. Most of us live at a certain level, and instead of understanding that we're living below what we're capable of, we make that level of alignment our identity and then continue thinking and acting in ways that reinforce that limited identity. Like if someone is living at a 5, they probably wouldn't say, "I'm living at a 5 right now, but I know I can let go of things that are heavy or move toward things that are expansive and start to live more in alignment with life." Instead, they have a belief that life is hard and no awareness of why it's hard. Take in right now that you're creating the awareness in yourself that is helping to remove the beliefs that have been creating a cycle of addiction to your old story.

Okay, so now that you have your AAA score, you've got a list of things in your life that are either above your average score or shrinking you and pulling your average down. Now take a look at the list and circle or put a little mark next to anything that is below your average. If you're still not doing this exercise and are just skimming to find out when it's over, realize that you won't know what your AAA score is and will have a harder time changing your life.

So anything that you circled or put a mark next to, those are suitcases that you are holding on to. Why are you holding on to those things? What fear inside of yourself are you running away from that is causing you to lower your value and stay stuck? Again, I'm not saying that you need to quit your job or leave your relationship just because it's below your average, but you should at least look at why you are holding on to those things. It's completely possible that, as you discover and accept whatever pain might be causing you to hold on to something, you completely transform your perspective of that thing. None of this is really about the external thing that you're doing—something that is a 1 for one person could easily be a 10 for someone else—it's about how we're relating to it and what level of awareness we have around it.

For example, someone could have a job that is a 3, which is below their AAA average, and instead of quitting without examining it, they could realize that they've been staying at that job and in resistance to it because of a story from childhood that says they are not good enough. If they sat with those feelings of unworthiness for long enough and felt themselves transcend their old story, it's possible that they could go back to that job with an entirely new perspective and a new version of themselves. It could feel completely different. They might bring a new level of creativity and productivity to the job and find themselves getting raises and promotions, which might make the job feel expansive and raise their alignment with it.

They could also quit that same job, fall into fear about not paying the bills, and instead of truly facing and accepting the fear and pain that is coming up from the story of their unworthiness, distract themselves with another habit or addiction that still keeps them from actually transcending their pain. This is not growth. Just leaping out of the thing that is heavy is not true transformation. It's the same pattern of not facing a fear that is looking for love and acceptance.

So this isn't just about running from one heavy thing to another without experiencing an internal shift. *This is about actually transforming ourselves.* Leaving jobs might be a part of it. Releasing addictions might be another part of it. But those things also have to be joined with a true inner discovery of what it is inside of you that has been blocking you. Whether you're moving toward a 10 or letting go of a 1, you're going to have to experience a real transformation to support your new vibration. If you're going to take a leap, you have to be fully present with it and allow yourself to completely experience everything that happens in your body as a result. That is where the change happens. Sit with your fears. Be there for the pain. Become a space that can love the part of you that is feeling unworthy. Sit in silence. Let yourself actually experience the shift that is taking place. The bigger the pain, the longer you might have to sit. You might have to walk around with a boulder sitting in your stomach for a day or two. With your patient presence, it will begin to dissolve, and in its place will be a new level of freedom and clarity that will support higher-level callings and next steps.

So do this for yourself. Look at your list and spend some time examining, leaping, removing, and moving toward the things that are calling you into this new space of possibility.

## Action: Transforming Your AAA Score

Go through the things that you have on your list. See if you can spend the next few days without one of the lowest-rated things in your list. If it's something like overeating or watching TV, see what it would be like to not do it, or do it less, for the next couple of days. If it's a person who's in your life, try spending less time with them for the next day or two. Also, take one of the things that you rated the highest and emphasize that thing. Do more of one of your 9s or 10s. After a few days, calculate your average again. Even if it just went up one point, from a 5 to a 6, realize that continuing that pattern for the next year would put you into a completely different life that would be a much clearer reflection of what you actually are. For extra credit: calculate your AAA score every Sunday for a year and see what happens.

# CHAPTER 10

# HOARDING YOUR PAST

I get it. It can be hard to move past our habits and let go of things that might have been in our lives for decades. It's easy to read about letting go of your old story and stepping into something new, but actually doing it is a completely different thing. If you're finding it difficult to imagine yourself letting go of the things in your life that aren't 10s, it's only because there's an attachment to your history that is stopping you from accessing your real power. Often, the reason that we hold on to destructive old stories, habits, addictions, people, and patterns from our past is because we haven't been able to accept, appreciate, learn from, and release our history so that we can move into full alignment with the moment. There's a huge difference between appreciating your history and hoarding your history—and it's a giant part of what is blocking us from our abundance.

We often make decisions based on our history instead of what our heart actually wants right now. For example: Do you live where you live because you actually want to live there right now, or because you've lived there for a long time? If you didn't live anywhere right now, would you choose to live in the same place? If you weren't dating or married to anyone right now, would you choose to start dating the person you're with? Would you apply for the job you currently have if you didn't already work there? Would you buy all the exact same food in your cupboards again if for some reason it completely disappeared?

Many of us are riding off of the momentum of what we did yesterday and allowing it to cut off the fresh, inspired desires that our heart has for us when we open to possibilities. We're hoarding our history, storing it inside our nervous system, and chasing some past emotional high instead of allowing ourselves to be brand-new in this moment and opening up to something bigger than we've experienced. Our mind often thinks that the best possible thing we could experience in this moment is only the re-creation of the best thing that has ever happened to us.

People are out there with huge boxes of mementos from past lovers, trying to reexperience the passion that they felt when they first met that person. Their mind is trying to relive that feeling because it can't comprehend the possibility of something better than that happening right now. I know someone who actually still gets a magazine subscription that someone they were in a relationship with used to have just so they can feel like they're still around in some way. Their house is filling up with all of these unwanted magazines so they can hang on to the experience they used to have with that person. There are new things to experience that are being blocked because they are clinging to what used to be. Their mind is putting them in lack because that past experience isn't currently happening. Instead of hoarding our past and living in lack, we can learn to appreciate our past—appreciate the expansion and depth that we gained from an experience or a relationship—and allow that appreciation to bring us into a new, open state of receiving that might attract a better, more amazing experience.

I'm not saying we need to delete all our past experiences or throw out mementos we might have of people that we've loved, but mentally holding on to things that make us feel lack in this moment is stealing our abundance and isn't truly honoring those experiences and relationships. If you believe you're in lack because of a lost lover, a lost career, a lost bank account, or anything that you think you've lost, you cannot be abundant in this moment. It doesn't matter how much money you have or how much external abundance you might have around you—if you are reaching for something in the past that you think you need to be complete, you are blocking the experience of real abundance from coming through. You are an infinite being who has the capacity to receive on an incredible level, but you can't receive if that space is already filled with the belief of lack.

This reminds me of an amazing client that I recently worked with named Mark. For years, Mark had been a caretaker for his parents as they were aging. He dedicated a big part of his life to taking incredible care of both his mom and dad up until they died. He was a caretaker for them for so long that even after they died, he remained in the identity of their caretaker. He was so programmed to take care of them, that once they were gone, he had no idea what he wanted for himself. They were his main source of connection, and even though they weren't around anymore, he was still looking for connection through them. Subconsciously, going after what he truly wanted would be demolishing the mental connection and attachment to the caretaker part of himself that got approval from his parents.

So Mark had an old Airstream trailer that he lived in. I had asked him at one point what he really wanted to do next with his life, and he immediately said that he'd love to travel to Europe and go to Paris. I could feel a real excitement there that seemed to me like it was beyond the story that he had been living in. I asked him why he hadn't gone, and he said he couldn't afford it. The more we talked, the more I discovered that there were many things in his life—like the Airstream trailer and a huge truck he needed to tow it—that weren't nearly as exciting to him as taking a trip to Europe and were actually keeping him from following a calling. I asked him if the Airstream was a 10, and he said, "Well, I have to have the trailer." I said, "That wasn't my question. I asked if it is a 10 to your body. Does it feel good? Does it expand you? Is it something your soul wants right now? Are you living where you want to live?" The more we did the work, the more he discovered that, no, the Airstream wasn't something he actually wanted. It was only the caretaker part of him that loved the Airstream. The deeper we went, he eventually realized that he had bonded with his dad over Airstreams, so he was really keeping the Airstream as a way to keep the connection with his dad going, while blocking himself from what he truly wanted.

When he looked into it, Mark found out that he could sell his Airstream for over $20,000, and he could sell the truck he used to tow it for $15,000. So, if he wanted, he could immediately have $35,000 to travel anywhere in the world. The realization that he could actually choose to sell that stuff opened up an entirely new door to start looking at other things that he had that weren't 10s. Another thing he had was an inherited rifle that a distant relative had used in the Civil War. I asked, "What if you sold that too?" He said, "Well, I have to keep it; it's a family heirloom." I said, "Do you? Who is making you keep it? Is it a 10 in your life?" The more he looked at it, the more he realized that keeping the rifle was more of a burden than an exciting calling. He was holding on to it in order to keep that same mental connection to his family going. I asked what he thought his great-great-great grandfather who used it in the Civil War would say about selling it. He felt into it for a second and then looked me in the eye and said, "I guess he would say something like 'Look, Mark, I'm dead . . . I don't even know what rifle you're talking about; I've been dead for a hundred years." I cry-laughed for like ten minutes after I heard that. It might be one of the funniest moments that I've ever witnessed. Here's this guy who has been holding on to all of this stuff that he thinks other people will be disappointed about if he lets it go, and the moment he looks at it from their perspective, he realizes they don't actually give a shit. It was his own mental attachment to his family's approval that was causing him to keep everything, not his family.

Some people might think that rifle needs to go to a museum, but why? So other people can look at another Civil War rifle from hundreds of years ago? Or would it be better for him to keep handing it down the line and giving generation after generation the burden of continuously moving this giant thing from the 1800s all over the place? And why is the thing that he used to murder people with the thing he's supposed to be remembered by? Why not pass down a nice blanket of his? Obviously I'm not a big Civil War history buff—maybe I'd feel differently about it if I were—but my point is, you don't always have to hold on to all of these external things to stay connected to your history. Your history is in you. Often, when we're using an external thing like an Airstream or rifle to stay connected to a parent or to your great-great-great grandfather Leonitus, we're not actually connecting to them; we're connecting to our mental assumption of their expectations of us. We're staying connected to an *idea* instead of allowing ourselves to find a real connection to them through our heart. When the mental attachment falls away, we move into our heart. When we're in our heart, we're connected to everything. We're connected to ourselves, which is our portal to connecting with everyone, even our ancestors. I'm not going into a weird ghost thing here; I'm just saying, what's weirder: trying to stay connected to someone through a rifle that we hang on the wall, or finding a true connection with *ourselves* that allows us to actually appreciate and honor them in this moment? They don't need us to keep their guns and old uniforms in a storage unit to feel connected to us. That's our shit we're carrying around, not theirs. That's our fear of not being loved, our fear of not getting approval, our fear of unworthiness.

I hope that my daughter doesn't feel the need to carry around all my old Huey Lewis records when I'm gone— or my bowling ball named "the Beast" or my VHS copy of *The Jerk* or my hot sauce collection featuring Dave's Insanity Sauce. That would be such a burden of me to expect my daughter to remember me at that level of spiciness. Although it could completely be a 10 for her to hold on to my Huey Lewis records, and it should be, because Huey Lewis is a 10 (musically).

So back to Mark—after that revelation, he now realized that he had a potential huge sum of money that he could put in the bank and move anywhere and live for quite a while. But, more importantly, he could undo this dramatic tie to his false identity and free himself to be alive in this moment. What would that do for his health, his enjoyment, his security (his *inner* security), and his freedom? He is only holding on to those things because he thinks they need to exist forever. When you realize that every single thing in the world is temporary, you stop holding on to things as much and go for experiences instead. An experience can expand you. An experience can move you into a whole new world and free you. Mark has always wanted to go to Europe—in my opinion, the last thing he would want to do is go to his deathbed and realize he never got to experience Paris because he held on to these old things that don't really bring joy to him.

So, as he released more and more attachment to the story of who he thought he was, Mark decided to take the leap and go to Paris. He told me that when he got back on the plane after the trip, he realized that he could now die happy. He said it was the most fulfilling experience of his life and shared with me that he visited all of these places he had only dreamed about and was constantly being moved to tears at how beautiful everything was. He said that he had never felt more alive than he did while he was answering that calling inside of himself and finally doing this thing that he has wanted to do for decades. Imagine what that means for him in all areas of his life. Think about the new dimension he has opened up for himself now that he doesn't see himself as someone who is limited by what he perceived as a lack of resources.

One of the reasons that we hold on to our history and our old way of being is because we don't have any idea what is on the other side of it. For instance, like Mark, if you're focused on the loss of something, you could be inches away from the greatest breakthrough you've ever had and completely miss out on what's right around the corner. It's like drilling for oil. Until you've actually struck oil, you don't know if it's there. The painful stories of our past aren't just there to make us feel sad or angry or repressed; they are there to take us deeper and uncover a bigger part of ourselves. When you give that pain the space and attention it needs, you keep drilling deeper, and eventually it will lead you to an entirely new perspective and the ability to connect to what you are on a new level.

You have no idea what is waiting for you when you untangle yourself from all the past regrets, disappointments, things that you are trying to re-create, and everything that is blocking you from right now. There is magic here when we don't try to shove all the remnants of our past into this moment. Appreciate your baggage, then release it and allow yourself to show up fully in this moment—you'll discover an entire new life full of possibility and abundance right in front of you.

---

## Action: Release, Rinse, Repeat

*Practice: Think about all the things you have in your life that are based on the momentum of your past. Take a look at all the things that you have in your house that no longer expand you—are there things in your closet or your garage or your attic that are only there because you have had them for a long time and you have a history with them? Are there people in your life who drag you down, but you're still friends with them because you've known them for twenty years? Take at least ten minutes to write down as many things as you can that are in your life because of a decision you made in the past that no longer ex-*

*cites you. Then, let go of at least one thing that you put on this list—whether it's donating that thing, energetically saying good-bye to someone, or canceling a subscription—notice the space that opens up in you when you let go of some of the weight from the past and make room for life to show up in a new way. Pay attention in the next couple of days and weeks to what shows up to take the place of that thing you let go of. When you notice what shows up to replace it, you can let that be a sign of what happens when you live in the practice of constantly releasing your past and become a space to receive the abundance of the moment.*

# CHAPTER 11

# FALLING IN LOVE WITH YOUR EXPANSION

As we receive this new paradigm, we're no longer aiming for money. Your awareness is too high to aim for the secondary thing. We now know that money is secondary. Who gives a shit about money? Seriously. You are so much more than money. You are all of it. You are the primary thing. You are expansion, growth, freedom. When we're aiming for our expansion instead of money or some temporary external result, we have a power and an intention that is thousands of times stronger than when we're trying to achieve some mental goal. Thousands of times might be an exaggeration, or it might be too little, I'm not sure. I guess it depends on the situation.

Even when we think we're trying to get something external, what we're really looking for is *internal* expansion.

External goals can also give us expansion, but only when they are on our highest edge and taking us beyond ourselves. When we fall in love, we're feeling expansion because we're experiencing a connection to someone else and ourselves that is new, but then we often get addicted to the person instead of the expansion that we felt. If you know that it's actually the internal expansion you are after, then you can continue your expansion by growing and allowing the relationship to evolve into something new. If you think it's the person or the time or the place where you met, then you will be addictively clinging to those circumstances and wanting that person to stay the same instead of encouraging them to grow into their next highest level of expansion.

This is a normal thing for most of us—we often experience expansion in some area of our life and then addictively look for that same experience over and over in the same thing, even though we are no longer getting expansion from it. I've talked before about going raw-vegan for ninety days and losing a ton of weight and feeling amazing—when I did that the first time it was a massive expansion for me and was death to the old story of the little kid who got love from his mom by eating burritos at Taco Time. I felt amazing and completely alive in a way that I had never experienced. After I finished that challenge, I was looking for that same feeling of expansion, so I decided to do it again, and I declared that I was going raw-vegan for another ninety days—but I didn't feel the same way. I wasn't expanding. I had already done that. Doing the same thing I had already done was not my next step. I didn't lose as much weight or feel the same kind of energy that I did the first time. Although eating extremely healthy was a factor, I believe the main factor in the results that I got the first time was that I was shedding the story of who I was and stepping into a new level of freedom within myself.

It was as if the first time I went raw-vegan, I was in third grade, learning whatever tactics I needed to get to fourth grade, but the second time I went raw-vegan, I was in fourth grade, still trying to use third-grade tactics to get to fifth grade. The old tactics weren't effective anymore because I was in a higher grade—I needed to learn a new way to expand myself beyond where I was.

Your expansion is your life force. If you're not expanding, you're contracting, you're constricting, you're dying. This is why identifying and stepping into your 10s is so important. When you're not choosing and moving toward the things that are exciting and expanding you, you're getting farther away from your connection to what you really are and sinking deeper into your mind-made limitations that are looking for an external circumstance to make you feel a certain way. If you're not expanding into something new, you are holding on to an out-of-date illusion and falling out of sync with a universe that is constantly moving forward.

When you move toward your expansion, you will get what you need—trust me. You will be provided for in some way that you can't see on this side of your mental assumptions, which can only see one or two linear ways to make something happen. You live in a universe with so much improbable and inconceivable shit happening. Dinosaurs were a thing. iPhones are a thing. The movie *Paul Blart: Mall Cop 2* is a thing. None of us could have guessed that the movie *Paul Blart: Mall Cop 2* would exist, but it does. I think that's all the proof you need to understand that life has possibilities available to you that are way beyond what your mind can see.

Okay, I realize you may need more proof.

Seriously though, it's ridiculous how much we doubt what is possible when there is a world around us that is filled with things that are seemingly impossible. How the hell does a tree work? Can you make a tree? I can't. How do you make a caterpillar? I have no idea. *So why do we think that we have to mentally strategize and be the sole creator of the possibilities in our life?* It's a little egotistical. Actually, it's completely egotistical. It's the ego that is cutting us off from the endless creativity that is wanting to collaborate with us. It's our ego that says we're not okay right now. It's the ego looking for something outside. It's the lifetime of experiences, old memories, inherited patterns, and societal beliefs stored in our minds that are tricking us into believing that what we want is a thing in the world outside, and not the expansion toward our soul.

Even though I've been drilling in the concept that we're not looking for something external, I actually believe that our calling can be both internal *and* external. Our expansion can be both an *internal* growth that allows us to connect with ourselves more deeply, and it can also be something that is expressed *externally* in the world. Our internal growth is something that is also meant to be shared with the world. That's why I say that when you aim for your primary expansion, you will be taken care of. When you aim for your primary expansion and access a new level of yourself, you're also probably going to feel an impulse to share it with the world. You've accessed a new level of value and expansion, and since the world is constantly moving toward greater and greater expansion (it's literally expanding faster than the speed of light), it will want to bring that new expansion to the world through you in some way.

So when I say that "you're taken care of" by aiming for the expansion instead of the thing, I'm not saying that you're magically going to get a Corvette—although that may also be possible—what I mean is, once you've created an expansion within yourself, that new space inside of you will be filled with an inspired idea, a piece of artwork, a new collaboration, or something that is an expression of this new awareness that has shown up in you. There may be some magical aspect to this that I don't know about, but what I'm talking about here has been my experience every time I've let go of mental chasing and stepped into my highest intention.

This is such a powerful concept and is really the way of being that this entire book is describing and moving us toward. It's moving into the infinite. It's moving exponentially. It's clearing out the programs that say what is and isn't possible. It's creating outcomes that we carry with us for eternity instead of the fifteen minutes it takes for the excitement of getting a new TV to wear off. It's accessing a new aspect of ourselves that can work in partnership with our minds to create on a level that is so much bigger than we're used to. It's learning to use our minds as a tool to translate the infinite callings of our soul instead of blocking them. It's connecting to our bodies and growing our antennas so that we can pick up higher ideas and insights. It's allowing something bigger than our limited vision of ourselves to emerge. It's *actually* evolving.

This world of being connected to what you actually are is getting closer, but your mind is likely still holding on to outcomes and goals in the external world. Your mind might have even been creating an external outcome as you read the last few pages, and if it was, that's fine—you're here to love that and release resistance to every part of yourself. Only through love can you transcend how your mind might be holding on to the promise that once you move toward the calling of your soul, then you'll have more creativity and more ideas that you can use to make more money or have more success. That's still chasing money, even if it's through the back door of connecting to the calling of your soul. If you decide to surrender the part of your mind that is constantly checking to see if the external results are showing up, you will start to access a powerful intention that is *bigger* than your goals.

A goal is something you can understand. An intention is defining and aiming toward an expansion. A goal is in the future. An intention is in this moment. A goal is an outcome. An intention is an internal direction. An intention is saying that you want to discover more of what you are, and that you're totally open to the fact that you don't know what the hell it is. A goal is "I want to make a million dollars." You know what a million dollars is, so that's not an exciting mystery that is going to cause you to leap into an unknown new level of yourself. When you have a defined goal, it actually can sometimes cap you at that level and prevent you from going deeper because you are attached to that external outcome. With an intention, you are surrendering the results and going into a deeper place that has no defined outcome—but it has an infinite amount of possibilities.

Having a specific external goal is like walking around with an oversize beach ball and trying to walk through doorways but constantly getting stuck. You have to look for the one doorway that can fit you and your beach ball at the same time. Having an intention is like having a nicely packed, uninflated beach ball that allows you to walk through many different-size doors and then blow up your beach ball when the time is right. A goal limits you to the one opportunity that you have mentally defined ahead of time. Your intention gives you the freedom to discover yourself and leaves you open to many opportunities that might match and support the new awareness that is emerging. And because you are discovering more of yourself, when an opportunity shows up, you're more aligned and able to take advantage of that opportunity.

So instead of capping ourselves at the level of our mind's goals, if we allow ourselves to go inward because we want to learn more about ourselves, we will learn to surrender to the flow of life and let it show us something better. Your mind understands goals; your heart understands a feeling, an intuition, an insight. Your heart is leading you to something that is *so much bigger* than whatever your goal is. No matter how big your goal is, it's nothing compared to what life is wanting to show you and bring into the world through you. We have to be motivated by an *inner intention* instead of our external goals, otherwise we'll be a slave to those goals and will miss out on the opportunity to truly express ourselves, create massive value, and shift the planet.

For example, if you start any type of creative project, let's say it's writing a book, but you don't have an inner intention for why you are doing it, then your mind will latch on to the need for a specific outcome and ask questions like "How can I write a book that people will like?" or "What sells?" If you're not leading with an inner intention that is driving you forward and listening to the inspired creativity of your heart, you'll be a victim to the external results and opinions of other people. If instead, you have a powerful intention like discovering patience and evolving more into what you are, then you're creating on a new dimension beyond what already exists in the world, you won't be as affected by other people's opinions, and you have the potential to create something truly groundbreaking.

If I were writing this book because of an external result, I wouldn't be able to do it. I'd be cut off from my soul, and it would be torture trying to figure out what I should write next, hoping that I do it right so that I can get something. I'd be completely drained, and it would take me forever. Instead, every day when I sit down to write I have a powerful inner intention of unfolding into more of what I am and creating a deeper connection to myself and the wisdom that is coming through. As a result, I'm writing this entire book in like a month, while also doing all sorts of other stuff. That's only possible because my intention for doing it is my primary goal. *I want to see what I become* more than I want to see what I get from it.

I've discovered recently that this is a natural way that I move, without really being fully aware of it. The things that I do are almost always entirely motivated by an inner intention that is moving me forward and taking me to a deeper place within myself. For example, I recently committed to a six-month-long coaching program with fifty people where we spend an hour on a video call together every morning at 6:30 A.M. This was so exciting to me, not because of any external result, but because of what it would cause me to become by making that level of commitment. I'm completely used to showing up at a theater, talking to an audience for a couple of days, and then taking off. I wanted to see how much I would need to evolve in order to hold space for fifty people, and myself, for an entire six months. Of course there were exciting external reasons, like how much everyone would shift over those six months, but the thing that was giving me the ability to actually commit to it was the mystery of what I would have to let go of and step into because of it. If my drive were only based on the external result of their transformation, then I'd be a slave to whether or not they were transforming and wouldn't be able to be as good on the calls because I would be cut off from my natural flow.

So think about some of the external goals in your life that you've been aiming for recently. These might be things like earning more money, creating a new business, finding a relationship, losing weight, buying a home, attracting new clients, etc. Think of the things that you've been aiming for outside and notice what it feels like in your body when you think of trying to accomplish them solely for the external result—it might feel exciting mentally, but if you're not connected to a deeper purpose, it's probably not a 10 to your body. If you can connect to an inner intention underneath those things and make *that* your primary goal, then those things might actually start to feel closer to 10s—or maybe you won't want to do them at all because your inner intention will discover something more exciting to take their place.

Think about how many times in your life you've had an external goal and then how, once you finally achieved it, you were happy for a couple of hours or days and then went back to chasing something else. We're going to start to replace those temporary circumstantial goals with an inner intention that isn't conditional. Your inner intention doesn't depend on circumstances. Your inner intention doesn't depend on whether people approve of you or not. Your inner intention doesn't compete with the external world.

Your inner intention is also something you can tap into *right now*—it doesn't take time or planning or money or a committee. If your inner intention is to connect to yourself more, you can start doing that immediately. Often, the only thing that is blocking us from living in our inner intention is chasing an external goal. When you allow your inner intention to become more important than your external goals, you start to align with a higher purpose. Your inner intention is your purpose in this moment. If your inner intention is to feel freedom, you can live your purpose by learning to experience your inner freedom now and transcending the mind-based belief that you are not already free. So what is *your* purpose right now? To discover true peace? To embody love? To let go of your past story? To go beyond what you used to be? Maybe your purpose right now is to listen and let life show you an intention.

When you do anything, if embodying your inner intention is your primary goal, you will notice an entirely different excitement and power behind what you do. You could be a shoe salesman and change your external goal of selling shoes to an inner intention of embodying peace—and your job selling shoes could now become a spiritual practice that is evolving you beyond yourself. Or your inner intention to discover peace could lead you into an entirely new career—either way, connecting to and following that intention will guide you into creating the circumstances in your life that will support your intention. If your inner intention is freedom, and you stay more connected to that than your external goals, you'll start to make choices in your life that lead you to more freedom. If your intention is to discover yourself, you'll start to move in a way that provides you more and more opportunities to discover what you are.

So you've probably already been thinking of what *your* inner intention might be—it should be a short, simple phrase that feels like the next step in your evolution. If you don't have one yet, take some time now to sit and allow it to come through. You can't mentally find your intention, so don't make this a job. It's something that will show up, if you let it. It could be to embody your feminine energy or your masculine energy. It could be to live in your truth. It could be to follow your heart. It could be to learn patience. It could be to express yourself fully. It could be to discover miracles. It could be to align with true creativity. It could be to live in the moment. It might be a combination of things. It might be to experience life without judgment. Your inner intention will feel like a 10—you'll know it as soon as it shows up. You've likely spent years moving toward external goals and ignoring an inner intention that has been dying to come through, so take this one moment to meet your intention and start your journey with it.

To actually embody your intention, your nervous system now needs to experience this shift by taking aligned actions. What changes do you need to make so that your body feels congruence between your new inner intention and what you are doing in the world? Is there anything in your life you could do today that embodies your inner intention? Maybe it's one of your 9s or 10s? Or is there any way to bring your purpose into the things you are already doing? Can you bring in your inner intention as you read this book?

Meditate because you have an inner goal to become more of what you are. Create because you want to discover the infinite creativity within you and connect to flow. Exercise because you want to connect to patience and intention. Do things based on the gravitational pull of your soul instead of a temporary fixation on an external result. Work from in to out instead of out to in. Become a creator instead of a consumer. Live from this powerful intention that allows you to transcend the mental habits and addictions of an insane society that is obsessed with material things. There is an entire universe inside of you waiting to be discovered, and when you find it, it will move through you and into this world with a creative power that you've never seen before.

## Action: Intention Deficit Disorder

*Whether your intention has shown up or not, spend thirty minutes to an hour sitting quietly and connecting to it or creating the space for one to show up. Don't try to find it—let it find you.*

# CHAPTER 12

# BECOMING YOUR INTENTION

Now that we've got our inner intention, or are at least open to it, we're going to make it our best friend. We're going to home in on what it means to live in our intention and learn to make it the most important thing in our lives. We're learning what it means to be more attached to the intention of our soul than the addictions of our mind. This is a feeling of being grounded and supported by something so much bigger than you.

Your intention is your superpower. It's what turns you from Clark Kent into Superman. When you connect to your inner intention, it's like finding the nearest phone booth and putting your cape on. All you have to do is shift yourself in a moment where you are pulled into the mental habit of chasing an external goal and move back into your intention—to experience freedom, to embody love, to express yourself—whatever it is. In any situation that is challenging, when you connect to your intention instead of the situation, you'll experience an entirely new level of strength.

For instance, if you're trying to quit an addiction like smoking or drinking or overeating, you're probably going to go through an experience of pain or sadness as you let go of the part of yourself that is addicted to the external results that you get. If you're living in the world of external results, then when you try to quit, you're going to be focused on the pain of not getting the results that you're used to. You'll likely either go back to the habit or find some other addictive external thing to fill the gap of the results that your mind is craving. However, if you have a strong inner intention like "to discover more of yourself," then the process of letting go of that addiction is actually in alignment with and supported by your intention. You would be discovering all sorts of things about yourself as you notice all the attachments and ways that you got love from that addiction. You might actually realize that you were in that addiction as a way to connect to yourself anyway, and as you discover that, you might also realize that you can create an even more direct connection to yourself without the addiction.

Your intention holds a loving and secure space for you as you go through challenging moments. It carries you through times where your mind might be looking for something to numb the pain. Your intention brings you a perspective that can see beyond the momentary pain of letting go of an old story and helps guide you into your highest alignment. It's a constant reminder of what you're actually aiming for and helps to remove the mental distractions that are trying to get your attention.

Your intention focuses your attention. Your intention is what allows you to give your full attention to your creativity. It allows you to give your full attention to love. It allows you to give your full attention to joy. Your intention blocks out the mental noise that separates you from what you are. Your intention *is* what you are. It's your truth. It's your real voice cutting through the chaos of the mind and powerfully saying, "No more Oreos—I want to fucking thrive!" It's lifting you off the couch and taking you on walks in nature. It's working through you and bringing real creativity to your work. Your intention is you. It's the real you.

So don't say that you *have* this inner intention—you *are* your inner intention. You are *discovery, freedom, love, joy.* You are *miracles,* you are *life.* Feel free to change your legal name to this new intention that you have. I know, in the past, I would have made fun of someone who changed their name to Miracles Johansson to match his new spiritual realization, but not anymore. I get it now, and I promise I won't make fun of you for doing that.

What would happen if you actually started to live as your inner intention? What would it be like to be *peace* instead of decades of old stories of unworthiness and regret? What would it be like to be *freedom* instead of all the patterns that your parents and ancestors handed down to you? What would it be like to be *abundance* instead of the worry of not being enough?

This is a completely different paradigm. This is living *as* something instead of chasing something that you think will *maybe help you feel a little better for a little while sometime in the future.* Do you see how insane that is and how many layers away from truth it is to live in a chasing mind-set? When you're chasing, you're trying to get a feeling through something external that will only temporarily make you feel the way that you want to feel. We need to stop looking for the cheap substitute of something that we already have. This is like having a billion dollars in the bank but obsessively buying *Monopoly* sets so that you can get the fake paper money. *You are already what you are looking for.*

So, can you see how abundance will be an obvious side effect of living as this inner intention you've created? Can you see how everything can be different when you are embodying more of what you are? Can you see how the mental addictions and habits that have been wasting your time and money and energy will start to fall away as you allow your inner intention to carry you into more alignment?

If you're feeling this, then understand that you are changing channels—you are moving out of the way that society has programmed you to live and stepping into an entirely new reality with an infinite amount of possibilities. When someone is living in their inner intention, they are unstoppable. You are unstoppable. This is going way beyond creating a life of abundance. That's obviously going to happen now that you have this level of awareness of what you are. We're now stepping into our world-changing levels. We're now going to a place where the by-product of becoming more of what we actually are will impact everyone around us, and maybe the world.

You are meant for this. If you've gotten this far, you are reading and understanding and feeling a book that is a call to everyone out there who is open to discovering what they actually are. You are extremely special. You are one of the few people who has the vision to see a life of possibility outside of what's on TV. You are transcending a lifetime of what you are not and stepping into a new dimension. On the other side of this is an entirely new life—but it takes *you* choosing it.

We're at the top of the roller coaster right now, and it's time to actually let go of everything that has been keeping us tied to our mental addictions. It's time to switch seats with our mind and allow our intention to take over. Great job so far, mind. Thanks for everything. We'll take it from here. This is our internal revolution. This is freedom.

By the way, I was joking when I suggested that you should change your name to what your inner intention is, but what you *should* seriously consider is allowing your intention to replace the mental identity that you've been attaching yourself to. Most of us have created an unconscious identity that is tied to all of these things that we've been trying to get external results from—our business, our job, our bank account, our relationship, our achievements. We're unconsciously believing that those things are who we are. That's the source of our pain. The source of your pain is not that your business falls apart or that you lose your job or you break up with your partner—the source of your pain, in the past, has been that you weren't connected to an intention that understands that those external things aren't you. These things are falling apart to get you closer to your intention.

When you are embodying what you are, those things can come and go, and while it may be challenging at times, it doesn't cause you the same type of pain as when you were believing that a part of you was dying because your business was struggling. When we're identified with our external circumstances, it can literally feel like losing a limb when that thing goes away. When you are living in your intention and allowing *that* to be your identity, your arms and legs are not in danger.

As a thrilling new burrito-based example of this: recently, I went on a juice fast. On the day that I started, my fiancée, Christy, happened to go to the store and buy tons of food for me because I hadn't told her I was on a juice fast yet. Near the end of day one of my fast, which is exactly the point when my mind usually questions it all and tries to convince my body that juice fasts are stupid and dangerous, I discovered that she had bought me the best burrito in the world. As you know, I like burritos an unhealthy amount. So as you can imagine, this burrito that represents my mom's love that Christy had brought me was extremely tempting. Now, this also happened to be the day that the concept of *connecting to your inner intention instead of the external results* had shown up for me in a big way. I had realized that instead of the results that I had been looking for in the diets and exercise I was doing, what I needed to embody was the inner intention of learning *patience*. However, when that burrito showed up, I had an immediate result available to me that was so much more exciting to my mind than the idea of patience.

So I picked up the burrito and instantly felt all the pain of my old story coming to the surface. I wanted to eat that burrito so goddamn bad. But it wasn't me who wanted to eat it; it was the identity of the little boy who was trying to get Mom's love who wanted to eat it. In that moment, I remembered that what I am is patience, not the identity of my old story. I held the burrito in my hand and connected to my intention and felt all of what I used to be fall off of me. I actually started crying. I know this is probably one of the first times that an adult has cried because of a burrito, and many of my comedian friends are going to give me crap about this, but that's really how much my old story wanted that burrito—a crying amount. In that moment, my intention filled the space that my mental attachment to an old way of being was taking up, and that old way of being left through my eyes. Being patience instead of my old identity allowed me to step out of a habit that would have given me comfort for a moment, but would have also kept me in an addictive cycle and stuck in my childhood pain.

A few days later, I stepped on the scale, and instead of weighing less, I weighed more. What the hell? I had been fasting, passing on burritos, and working out like crazy. Then I remembered that my intention is patience and got excited that I was about to step into my inner intention and embody the patience of my soul even more. If my intention was named results, I would have been disappointed and upset, so I probably would have quit juicing and reheated that burrito—like I've done many times before. But in a space of being patience, I was in a completely different world. I stayed with it and learned so many things about myself that I didn't know I needed to learn. I wasn't disappointed; I was excited about what I was becoming. From this new channel, a completely different life began to unfold. An entirely new me was emerging just because of one stupid burrito.

What's your burrito? What's the thing that is calling to your old story that might lose its power in the face of you connecting to what you are? Maybe it's also burritos. Or maybe it's something else, which is much more likely, just based on the number of things that exist. Whatever it is that has been keeping you trapped in a story of limitation, just try embodying your inner intention and see what happens the next time you're feeling pulled toward it. This is big work. This is becoming the space that the story is in instead of the story. This is connecting to your universal self. This is expanding your awareness, big time. You won't believe the power that comes from looking an addictive habit in the eye and allowing all the illusional past parts of you to be replaced with the knowing of your higher purpose.

Don't just let this be a concept. Bring this into your body. Experience this. Practice this. Practice allowing your inner intention to override your unconscious mental attachments in the small moments, like with tacos, and it will be easier in the big moments, like with burritos. Everything that we do is us either being pulled toward the expansion of our soul or addictively shrinking into the mental story of who we've been tricked into believing we are.

It's like you're constantly on *Let's Make a Deal* and choosing between the door that your inner intention wants (door number one) and the door that your unconscious egoic identity wants (door number two). Your heart is constantly trying to get you to choose door number one, which has creativity and fulfillment and abundance and a new house behind it, but your mind is trying to convince you to pick door number two, which just has cold pizza and sadness behind it. When you listen to your old story and pick the door that has cold pizza and sadness behind it, you miss out on all the amazing things that were behind door number one, but you don't even know about that—you only know that you at least got the semi-joy of eating cold pizza. So whenever it's time to choose between the two doors again, your mind reminds you of that tiny amount of joy you got from the cold pizza and tells you how much you'll be missing out on if you don't pick that door again. We're constantly choosing cold pizza and sadness because of a fear of missing out on it—and ignorant of what is beyond it.

It always seems like we're missing out on something so much bigger than what we're actually missing out on.

Door number two for someone who smokes cigarettes is deciding to continue smoking, which gives them about five minutes of relaxation, a lifetime of decreased lung capacity, and a heightened possibility of cancer. Door number one would be *quitting* smoking, which would mean increased health, lower expenses, and the opportunity to stay in hotel rooms that have had fewer bachelor parties in them. Our minds are masters at persuading us to choose door number two, even when there are completely obvious downsides and only a tiny upside.

This world is on autopilot, constantly picking door number two and making us feel like we should too. It wraps door number two up in a bow and tries to convince us of how amazing it will be once we choose it. You only have to buy billboards for something if it is a door-number-two choice. You only have to hire a sexy model to promote something if it's not good for you. Nature doesn't have billboards. Meditation doesn't have infomercials. You never get interrupted during dinner by a telemarketer reminding you to spend quality time with your family. The truth doesn't need manipulation. The truth doesn't need tricks. It already fucking rocks. It's better than everything—it's the truth. You only need advertisements to make something that's not the truth look like the truth. It's fairly obvious what the door number twos of this world are, but somehow many of us are still being tricked into choosing the things that pull us away from what we are and into an addictive habit that closes us off from our soul.

There is so much abundance waiting for us if we stay connected to our inner intention, have a little faith, and start to pick door number one—even when it's painful and we know that we're going to miss out on something that gives us pleasure. There is something so much bigger than pleasure out there. There is something so much more fulfilling than distraction. There is something so much more permanent than external success. There is an unimaginable amount of abundance that begins to reveal itself when we stay in the intention to let go of our chasing mentality and allow life to fill us up from the inside. Replace your door number twos with door number ones, create a new identity that is connected to the vision and power that are available in this moment, and discover what you actually are in the process.

### Action: Let's See What's Behind Door Number One, Everybody!

*Spend a good chunk of time today or tomorrow in nature without any distractions—even if it's just a nearby park. Don't bring your phone. Pay attention to the way that nature moves. Notice how many things in nature will mirror your intention back to you. For instance, if your intention is patience, experience the way the trees are constantly embodying patience in every moment. If your intention is to embody true creativity, explore all of the infinite creativity that nature is using to do all that it does. Also, notice how many of your door-number-two egoic desires dissolve in the presence and truth that surrounds you in nature. Afterward, see how much you can bring those qualities of nature back into your everyday life to help strengthen and support your intention.*

# CHAPTER 13

# GIVING

Now that we're changing channels, removing heavy addictive patterns that keep us in a protective state, and discovering that we have a never-ending supply of what we've been looking for already inside of ourselves, our natural evolution is going to bring us more into the vibration of *giving*. That's just how it works. When you're living in your heart and you know that you have an abundant supply of what you need, you naturally want to share it with others. Giving is also a way to prove to yourself that you are abundant. When we're in the vibration of chasing, our general feeling is that we don't have enough, so we're in complete protection of what little we believe we do have—but that's not the way that life moves.

Life is constantly giving and sharing and collaborating with itself. The sun is constantly giving its light to the earth. The earth is always sharing its nutrients with the trees. Trees are naturally giving their fruit to the animals. Imagine an apple tree that is hoarding its apples because of a belief that it doesn't have enough. It wouldn't be able to make more apples because its branches are filled with old, rotting ones. In reality, the apple tree isn't afraid of running out of apples; it just creates them and lets them go. It knows that it has access to exactly as many apples as it needs. I'm not a botanist, so just know that this is a loose metaphor based on my general intuition about apple trees. I have no idea what they are thinking, but they seem pretty chill about their apples.

Giving is a way that you constantly renew yourself and stay connected more to your inner abundance than your mental attachment to external things. It can be so healing to give away a big chunk of money and allow the old identity that believed *it was* the money to fall apart. A huge shift for me in this area happened many years ago when I went to an event to raise money for kids in an undeveloped part of Africa to go to school—for every $100 that was donated, a child got to go to school for a year. I had donated to things in the past, but at this event, a voice showed up that was urging me to give beyond my usual level—I had this inspiration in my body that said, "What if we donated a giant amount of money?" I got insanely excited about donating $10,000 and giving a hundred kids a year of education. It was a feeling that was inspiring to me. I wasn't doing it to get anything; it just felt good to support what they were doing. So I followed that calling, leaped, and donated $10,000. (I know this story could sound like it's bragging, but I am really just telling you this so I can show you what happened when I gave beyond my perceived limitations. But yeah, I'm pretty great.) Giving that money felt scary, because it was a lot for me, but it was also extremely exciting. I could feel in my body that it was an action that moved me beyond myself and into more of the collaborative energy of giving.

At the time, I was performing at colleges as a comic and my rate was about $7,000. The day after I donated the $10,000, I got booked for a college that wanted to pay me $17,000—exactly $10,000 more than my typical rate. For some reason, they wanted to give me $10,000 more than I usually got. I'm not claiming that anything magical happened to create a situation where the money came back to me immediately, but I do know that in donating that money, it felt as if I were releasing a part of myself that had been chasing money and that I was making space for something bigger to come in. Energetically, it wasn't normal for me to give that much—I saw myself as worth less than that. But in giving that much, I saw myself open up and felt a higher level of value that brought in a faster-moving flow. So not only did the $10,000 come back to me the very next day, but there was something that shifted in me that made me realize how when you move into alignment with giving, you also move into alignment with receiving—which is a lesson that I know has brought back so much more to me than I donated. *Your ability to receive is equal to your ability to give, and vice versa.*

How much you can give is based on how much you understand that you are connected to the *source* of money rather than the money. I'm not saying you should give money away so that you can receive money, because that doesn't work. If you're giving just so you can receive, you're still energetically saying that you're in lack. Having said that, proving to yourself that you are the source of your abundance by giving beyond your old story can be a powerful way to release the part of you that has been blocking abundance from coming in. When you hand someone a check or give your time or your energy in a way that stretches you, you're literally handing over a representation of your old story and making room for a new reality.

When you do something like that, you're also doing something that is selfless, which actually means you are taking an action that has no "self" involved. If you want to expand into oneness with life and experience actual connection with what you are, you have to transcend the idea that there is any part of you that is separate from everything else. The idea of yourself as separate from the universe is an addiction, and it's not true.

Amazing opportunities will show up when you start to move to a place of selflessness. Even going for a walk and picking up trash for a few hours will start to get you thinking in a more universal way instead of in terms of your small story that has all of these problems to solve. Becoming selfless enables you to connect to a frequency that is higher than your problems, and it's also higher than everything that you thought you wanted. In a place of true selflessness, you'll find that you don't really want anything. It was just your small story that believed it was separate that wanted all of those things. When you connect to a feeling of not really needing anything to be happy (which frees you up to give even more), you actually become a massive space to receive because life knows you are a true participant in the circulation of abundance.

I understand that some people reading this might not feel like they have enough to give in the first place. I get it, but it could also be possible, in some cases, that we don't have enough to give because we haven't been giving in a way that puts us in alignment with receiving. We may have been in a protective state with our time and our energy and our money, and by doing that, we're telling ourselves that we're not enough—and life is matching that. When we see our ability to give as based on the amount that we currently have, we are capping ourselves at the level of our current story and living within our limitations. If you're saying that you can't give past your story, you're also saying that you can't *receive* past your story, so you're stuck there. Many people convince themselves that once they create money or success, *that's* when they will become generous and giving—but often it's the fact that they are holding on to and hoarding their money that is actually keeping them from being able to create abundance in the first place. We have to first move past the fear of letting go of our old story of limitation and into the energy of giving and selflessness, and *then* abundance will flow.

We're already being given so much in every moment. We're being given life, consciousness, oxygen, a planet, sunlight. There are so many gifts that allow us to be here right now. When we're giving to the world in whatever way we can, we're aligned with the same universal energy that is beating our heart. I know I've made some of these points, but I want to keep us in the habit of acknowledging the unbelievable gifts all around us so we can tap into an abundant energy that allows us to share even more. When we're sharing the abundance that we've discovered in ourselves, we're connected to what we are. We're moving beyond the mental barriers that keep us separate from ourselves and others, and stepping into a true sense of oneness with life. We're not just these separate beings who are competing with one another—our hearts are all beating because they are connected to the same thing, and we're here to help and support each other as we grow toward the next stage in our evolution.

Giving money to someone who truly needs it can feel so much better than buying more stuff we don't need. If you can see someone else as deserving of receiving, that's practice for you to see yourself as deserving of receiving. When you get to experience the joy that someone gets from receiving something bigger than they perceive themselves to be, you are saying to yourself that *you deserve to receive something bigger than you perceive yourself to be too*. I know that there's a part of our mind that might think we shouldn't give money to someone else because we earned it and they didn't. That's true on one level— that's the level of the disconnected mind that makes us feel separate and creates suffering. When I give money to a homeless person, I'm dissolving the barrier that says they are different from me. I get that they could use that money for an addiction or whatever, but that's not my business. My business is following the inspired calling of my heart, and my heart wants to share. It wants to give. It wants to let someone else know that they're not alone in this world, which tangibly proves to me that I am *also* not alone in this world. Instead of judging them for a life that I have no idea about, my heart wants to share a piece of the inner abundance that I've cultivated with someone else so that humanity can move forward and we can stop fighting one another. I know giving $100 to a homeless person isn't going to stop wars from happening, but if we all begin to move toward the vibration of seeing ourselves as all connected instead of separate, then maybe we won't be so concerned with holding on to and fighting for the money that seems to divide us.

Giving is one of the easiest ways to transcend the mental story that is telling us we need to get, that we need to protect, that we need to hoard. It's an action that rewires our nervous system and tunes our body to the frequency of possibility. Giving is an exercise in living in the moment and stepping out of past and future. Giving challenges everything that the mind has been trained to do. So I want to challenge you to give in a way that's at least one step beyond what feels comfortable or normal to you, and to start experiencing what it feels like to be a space where money and energy have the freedom to move through you without resistance. If you have a waiter or waitress who is really awesome, blow their mind by giving them something that is more than you've ever given. If you see someone who needs help, help them, spend time with them—do something that you'll never forget. It will feel so much better than just sitting at home watching a movie.

Of course, giving doesn't have to be about money. It can be your time, your presence, your expertise, your possessions, your creativity—but whatever it is, make sure you're giving in a way that is challenging your old story and forcing you to move into a deeper connection with your inner abundance and intention. Please don't give anything away that puts you at risk of defaulting on your mortgage or having your car repossessed. This isn't a game of chicken to see how much you "trust the universe." Just go one or two steps beyond what has been your normal range of giving and allow yourself to feel the way that your ego tries to justify why you shouldn't give that much. And make sure it's something that calls to you. It's not just in the donating; it's in the answering of a calling that is moving you toward growth.

Through the practice of giving, discover the ways that your mind has been keeping you from sharing what you have with the world. These are the same ways it's been keeping you disconnected from yourself and the infinite abundance inside of you. Stretch yourself and feel all the emotions that come up when you do. If difficult fears or emotions surface, realize that those are the ties to your old story that are being pulled out of your body as you attempt to give in a way that is bigger than your story. Beyond that pain will be a freedom and a space where a new level of creativity and abundance can show up.

Almost every person that I have ever met who gives in a big way is abundant. The people that I know who are extremely generous are often also the happiest. I'm not talking about people who give in a people-pleasing-type way, or in reaction to a taker. I'm talking about people who are giving from, and living in, an abundant energy versus a lacking energy. I'm talking about the people who have a grounded sense of internal abundance that makes them excited to pay for the meal, or not haggle over prices, or take time off work to be with a friend who needs them. These are the people who are living more in the connected space of their body instead of their rigid belief systems. These are the people who others also feel safe giving to. These are the people who others feel safe collaborating with. The people who are rooted in their own sense of abundance are the ones who are attracting other people who are connected to *their* inner abundance, so they often get together and collaborate to make even more abundance. So when you're giving to a homeless person or donating to a charity or volunteering at a retirement home, you're actually connecting to a network of heart-based people who are also living in their abundance. When you're holding something back out of fear and feeling like you don't have enough to give, you are creating a vibration of lack that a potential business partner may pick up on, which might cause them to not be excited to work with you. When you allow yourself to break the habit of lack and lean toward trust, you become a safe space of possibility for others to collaborate with.

One great lesson that showed up in my life about this actually came years ago when I was backstage with Jim Carrey after I had the honor of working with him and Eckhart Tolle at an event called GATE. I remember sitting with Jim for about twenty minutes backstage, and at one point, I said, "I sure would love to do a movie with you sometime." And he said back, "Then it will happen!" He said it in a tone that kind of sounded like "Trust. Keep growing. Don't worry about what you want right now. Just be you." After he said that, it dawned on me that what I was actually saying to him was, "I want you to put me in one of your movies."

Me saying that had nothing to do with collaboration, because I had much less to offer him than he had to offer me. I probably wasn't a safe space for him to give to me because I was not actually giving to him; I was asking for a handout. Because of that, there wouldn't be an equal reciprocation if he made a phone call and put me in one of his movies. It wouldn't be an easy flow. I asked under the guise of, "Let's work together," but in that moment, Jim Carrey had a higher alignment than I did—so the idea of working together didn't align.

As my career has grown, I've now been on the receiving end of that conversation many, many times. I have absolutely no judgment when this happens, but people often ask me for favors who also don't necessarily feel like they are in the alignment to receive what they are asking for. I'm open to working with anyone, and anyone can do the work of raising their alignment to a place where it feels effortless to collaborate with them, but I now know the exact feeling Jim Carrey had when I asked him if we could work together.

The feeling that Jim Carrey had with me, and the feeling that I now have with others who feel out of alignment, has nothing to do with Jim Carrey or me—it's a universal thing. That feeling is the universe saying, "Nope, it doesn't align right now." Rather than getting discouraged about an opportunity that you're not aligned with, get excited about the opportunity to raise your alignment. One major way that will happen is, instead of looking for opportunities to get something from others, start to look for opportunities to give to others *without expecting anything in return.*

The way that many of us have been taught to give is conditional—we're looking to get something from what we give. What I'm talking about here is giving on an entirely new level, not giving so we can receive—this is giving in a way that connects us to the world around us and allows life to work through us.

This is us serving life instead of just serving ourselves. This is us choosing to stop destroying the planet in a constant search for more and starting to move in a way that gives us a future. This is moving beyond the individual and into harmony with the whole. Giving is your opportunity to prove to yourself that your past does not determine your worthiness to receive and that you are bigger than your beliefs. Give in a way that stretches who you are a little more every day, and watch your world become a more giving place.

## *Action: Demolish Your Limitations*
## *by Giving Beyond Them*

*As discussed earlier in this chapter, do something that calls to your heart and would expand you beyond your small story that is in contribution to someone else or to the world as a whole. Whether it's picking up trash, spending time in a children's hospital, or writing thank-you cards to the people in your life, see if you can do something that causes you to give on a level that you've never given before. See if you can move to a place of selflessness as you look at the world through the eyes of the universe versus the eyes of your separated "self."*

# CHAPTER 14

# YOU OWN NOTHING, AND EVERYTHING

This might be shocking, but do you know that the money you have in your account isn't yours? Seriously. You don't own that money. I'm not saying you're a criminal or anything. I'm just saying that before that money was in your account, it was in someone else's, and eventually, you'll exchange it for something like a mini-trampoline or a commemorative plate collection, and it will be in someone else's account—probably the Mini-Trampoline and Commemorative Plate Collection Corporation of America's account. They pretty much have a corner on the market when it comes to both of those things.

Even though money is constantly being circulated through our society, we almost all have this subconscious way of acting like the money we have is ours and only ours. This belief that makes us feel like we own the money we have is *also* the thing that keeps all the other money in the world out of reach. The belief that we own our money creates an equal and opposite belief that we *don't* have access to all the other money in the world. Stay with me here for a second.

The more someone believes that they own the $2,000 that's in their bank account, and the more protective about it they are, the more they enforce the belief that the other trillions and trillions of dollars in the world are *not theirs.* It's like if you went to the beach, and instead of just enjoying all the sand around you, you wanted to own the sand. All you have with you at the moment is this one backpack, so you start shoveling as much sand as you can into it. Now you're wearing a one-hundred-pound backpack of sand and you can't move. You also can't take it off because you don't want someone to steal it. There are millions of pounds of sand all around you that you don't have access to because of your limited belief that you own what you have in your backpack. This is how we are with money. We trap ourselves in the box of what we currently have and cut ourselves off from the unlimited flow of abundance all around us because we don't understand that no one owns the sand—we're all just enjoying it for a little while.

What if you didn't believe that you only had the money in your account, and instead understood that you have access to *all* the money in the world? Well, you do. You have access to it all, and so does everyone else. When you embody that and release yourself from the small story of your current circumstances, you will start to elevate your perspective and create a value that aligns with all the abundance that is out there for you. The belief of ownership is a stagnant vibration of fear that prevents us from shifting into a dimension of flow where there is less ownership but more abundance and freedom for everyone.

The concept of owning anything is a completely mind-made illusion. By attempting to own something, we're trying to make that thing a part of what we are. The mind is constantly trying to build itself up by latching on to all of these things in the outside world so that it can protect itself. When we believe that we own something, we're saying that it's ours and nobody else's, and if someone tries to take that from us, they're attacking us directly. The idea of owning something actually makes us extremely vulnerable. It's like getting a new car and being obsessed with making sure that it doesn't get scratched. The first time that a new car gets scratched or dented can cause some people literal pain in their bodies. It's almost as if their own body got injured—sometimes worse. When we buy into the mind-made belief that we can own anything at all, we create an instant fear of losing what we believe we own—which feels like losing a part of ourselves.

I was talking to a friend recently who told me she doesn't buy expensive things because she is scared they could be scratched and damaged, and I asked, "Is that how you treat relationships too? Do you not want to have the ultimate relationship because you could lose it? Is that actually preventing you from receiving lots of money because you could lose it too?" She had a predetermined belief that she was going to lose something, which is likely preventing her from receiving it in the first place—which is the same as losing it, without the ability to at least enjoy it for the time that she would have had it. She's also missing out on all the growth that might have come with that experience.

How much is a belief of ownership unconsciously tying you to the belief that you might experience pain? What if undoing those fears brought you to a level of abundance where things can come and go without any pain at all?

*Owning* (and being afraid of losing what you own) is a complete contradiction to the vibration of *giving*. Giving requires releasing your attachment to the thing that you are giving, which allows you to expand into a bigger, more connected space. Owning creates a mental attachment to the thing, which creates a layer of separation between you and others because you're holding on to this thing and protecting it from the world. I'm not saying to not own stuff, and this isn't me making a case for communism or anything like that. I know we are still going to want to have a car and a home and clothes and the *Back to the Future* trilogy on Blu-ray. All I'm doing is pointing to a vibrational way of being that can allow us to move beyond the traditional way of looking at ownership, which is one of the main causes of suffering and one of the biggest reasons for basically every war that happens in this world.

For instance, the idea of owning a certain piece of land is a really strange thing that humans have come up with, and it's also one of the things that has caused the most violence on this planet. Fortunately, bears don't have the proper documents showing that they're the ones that actually own the land, otherwise we'd all be screwed. We think that if someone is standing on land that we own, that they are standing on us. But they're not standing on us; we're over here. We're not our stuff. We're not the people we date. We're not other people's opinions. We're *us*.

It's like breathing. If you took a breath and thought that you owned that breath—and wanted to make sure you don't lose that breath and that nobody else could have that breath—you'd have to hold your breath forever, and obviously, you'd die. In order to survive, our body is constantly bringing in what it needs and letting go when of what it no longer needs, which frees it up for someone or something else to use it. Water comes into our body and then leaves when it's time. Our skin and organs are constantly using the nutrients and minerals we get from the earth to renew themselves and then shedding their old cells so they can move back into the earth. One thing that I've heard is that every cell in the body is replaced every few years (don't take my word for this; I didn't finish college . . . and I'm too lazy to find where I heard this from). So if the body that we are living in isn't trying to hold on to itself for the rest of its life, then why are we trying to hold on to things that obviously aren't a part of us? This mental identification with the things around us is a kind of sickness that is pulling us farther and farther from the core of what we are.

Your car is a tool. Your phone is a tool. Your home is a tool. These are things that help us and protect us and keep us safe, and they're awesome—and if we're fortunate enough to have these things, we should be extremely appreciative—but there is a mental attachment to these things that can cause us to be owned by the very things that we think *we own*. This is a huge realization—anything that you own, *owns you*, at least in some small way. Everything we own is taking some amount of space in our mental world and causing us to feel tense because we are holding on to it on some level. We always have one part of ourselves keeping track of it, protecting it, insuring it, or mentally maintaining it. One reason why it feels so good to go on vacation and stay in a hotel room is because almost none of your crap is there—you've at least put some distance between you and the gravitational pull of all the things that you think you own. That's the real vacation. Could you imagine if you went to a hotel and it was two stories and came with an attic of old stuff that you had to sift through? How relaxing would that hotel be? You go there and there are five hundred boxes in the basement that you're ignoring. That'd be crazy right? Well, why would we *live* that way?

Often people think that freedom will show up when they have tons of money and can buy anything they want, but in many ways, it's the complete opposite. If you're buying things from the energy of wanting to own something so that you can become more, then you're adding more stuff to your *mental* identity, and it will likely cause you to become less connected to yourself and the freedom that you actually are.

We never really own anything; we're just borrowing it for a little while—and then either it's going to leave or we're going to leave. Under the belief of ownership, we're setting ourselves up to experience suffering because we believe we're losing something that is a part of us instead of being a space where the things in our life are free to come and go. Life becomes much easier when we understand from the start that nothing is ever ours forever. Nothing can come with us when we die—not our car, not our job, not our lover, not our body.

That's right—in many ways, you don't even own your body. Yes, it's your body, but your body is not what you are. Our body is something that we are experiencing. It's something that our consciousness is inhabiting, but it doesn't define us. If we lose an arm or a leg, that doesn't mean we're less of a person. Our consciousness, our value, our worthiness stays exactly the same.

We don't even own our thoughts. They're happening inside of our consciousness, but we don't own them. They come and go as they please too. You can't always

decide what thoughts you think. Have you ever been in a terrible mood and then had an annoying friend tell you to just think positive? Were you able to? No, you probably thought, "I don't like you anymore, Janice."*
*Janice is a fictional character I made up for this joke.

Where do your thoughts even come from? Do you actually create your thoughts? If so, how did you start creating thoughts? Did you learn about it on YouTube? I have no idea how my thoughts show up, so I don't take ownership of them. I know enough to realize that I have no idea where these thoughts are coming from, so why would I pretend that I own them or that they are what I am?

I am the space that my thoughts are in. I am the space that my body is in. I am the space that is aware of my car and the home that I live in. I am the space where a relationship with my fiancée is happening. I don't own any of those things, and none of those things are who I am. The only way that those things can exist in my life is by me being okay with letting them go. I have to be okay with the fact that my body is going to age. I have to be okay that I can't take this home with me when I die. I have to be okay with the possibility of my relationship falling apart—that's the only way that it can be a real space of freedom and actual love for both of us.

One of the strangest but most common things that we take unnecessary ownership of is other people's opinions. How many time have you changed your behavior based on the opinion or judgment of someone else? That's us taking their judgment (actually, our perception of their judgment) and making it part of who we are, and then keeping it alive inside of us as we mold ourselves into the person we think they want us to be. Sometimes we hold on to other people's opinions our entire lives and allow their perspectives about who we are to be even stronger than our own. If someone has an opinion about you, that's fine, but if you think it's your responsibility to do something about someone else's opinion about you, then you are owned by their opinion, which cuts off your own unique flow of expression that is here to bring massive value and abundance into the world.

There are many things that we take ownership of that cut us off from flow. For example, you might have debt, but you don't have to believe that debt is what you are. Yes, you have to own up to it and be responsible for it, but you don't have to carry the vibration of debt inside of you in a way that lets debt take over your entire being. You can be currently in debt but see it as something that is just passing through, like everything in your life.

Oftentimes we have the habit of becoming attached to whatever is happening in the moment and assuming that it will never leave. Whether we're in a high or a low, our mind often thinks that we're going to be experiencing this forever. When we're sad for more than a couple of hours, we start freaking out, thinking that something is wrong with us and we're never going to feel happy again. We think that when we're in debt, we're *always* going to be in debt. We think that when we're in a relationship, we're always going to be in that relationship. This is a mental construct that isn't listening to the truth about life. Everything in life is temporary. The sun is temporary. The Earth is temporary—hold on, I should look that up—okay, yeah, I found a few seemingly legit articles saying the Earth will eventually disintegrate in billions of years. So yeah, great news! Even this planet isn't here forever! Shit!

When we move into alignment with the truth of how this universe works, things start really moving for us and we begin to tap into some real power. When we let go of the need to own things or have experiences last forever, we make room for amazing things and experiences to come in so much faster. Even the best experience you can imagine having—if you could have it for the rest of your life—would still be blocking experiences that are even beyond that from coming in. So, with this new awareness, we can stop trying to own life and allow it to show up in all the unique and unexpected ways that it wants to. This kind of surrendering is unbelievably freeing. If you let go of having to manage everything in your life, then your life will be managed better than it ever has. This is letting it all go—and allowing it all to show up for you.

## Action: Congratulations, You Own Nothing!

*Sit for at least a half an hour with your eyes closed and allow yourself to think about all the things in your life that you think you own: your thoughts, your body, someone else's opinion, physical objects around you. Allow yourself to sit and notice all the thousands of different things that you may have once believed that you own but have actually owned you because of your mental attachment to them. You might have them, they might be in your consciousness, but they aren't you. Really allow yourself to do this before you move forward.*

# CHAPTER 15

# UNCONDITIONAL LOVE

Underneath the illusion of money, or our need to own something or to chase something or to find security in something outside of us—there's just love. When we're not in our head, planning or fixing or regretting something we've done, what shows up is love. That's what you really are—pure unconditional love. Love can be kind of a vague term that many people might associate with approval or attachment or dependency, but I see love as the feeling that we experience when we go beyond all the layers of ego that are seeing something as wrong with the world or someone else or ourselves. Unconditional love is love beyond the conditions of the mind.

To truly love ourselves is to experience ourselves beyond all the mental judgments, comparisons, inadequacies, and conditioned patterns of unworthiness that we've picked up from the world. Beyond how much money you make or what you've achieved or what you look like or how smart you are, there is an unconditioned part of you that is a perfect reflection of the infinite love of the universe. That's the point of this book. I'm not just trying to help you become more abundant—I'm standing outside of you, knowing that you are universal love and perfection, and I'm trying to help you to peel back the layers that have been covering that up. You're not looking for love; you *are* love. You're not looking for abundance; you *are* abundance. You don't have to look for anything. You can fall back into the truth of what you are and discover a source of power and completeness that has the ability to create a life that is abundant and fulfilling beyond your wildest dreams.

This chapter offers the opportunity for us to actually embody true, expansive, unconditional love—first for ourselves, and then for everyone and everything around us. When we move into a vibration of love, we move into harmony with the creative force of life that is constantly giving us more and more opportunities to step into what we are.

Truly loving ourselves is magical. When you can let go of the idea that something is wrong with you or that you need anything to be complete, something amazing happens. You meet up with truth. You sync up with the way that life is seeing you and allow it to pour its love and creativity and abundance into your world. You become an open space to receive all the love that the universe has to offer. You begin to embody a love that wants everyone to feel free. You become a space of love that doesn't want ownership of anything or anyone. You become someone who is creating instead of destroying, who is liberating instead of imprisoning, who is sharing instead of hoarding. You become a portal of love that can move this planet forward. You become a space of awareness that can help heal the world instead of contributing to its pain.

Real love doesn't control. Real love doesn't hoard. Real love doesn't own. Real love doesn't judge. Real love doesn't fix or argue. Real love just *is*. If you go into nature or just listen for a while and don't interrupt your evolution by checking your phone or your e-mail, this love is what is going to show up inside of you. You're going to see the parts of you that aren't actually you— all the controlling, owning, fixing parts of you—will start to go away. The essence of what you are will get louder. The expansive, loving, infinite part of you is always going to be there. The only thing that is afraid of going away is the false, egoic shell that causes all your pain and separation.

When you allow the parts of you that have been trying to control and manipulate life to leave, no one can control or manipulate you. You start to live in a higher awareness that is listening to your internal self-love, and what other people do or say doesn't affect you. If you're connected to the unconditional love that you are, then someone else's egoic judgment can't even reach you. It's on a different channel. Their judgment is on a vibration that can't compete with your powerful knowing and embodiment of love.

If you're looking for love from anywhere other than inside of you, then you're probably not looking for love. Most of us aren't seeking love from others—we are seeking approval, control, ownership, and attachment. You can never find love that you are missing inside of yourself in someone else. People can only truly love you at the level they love themselves. The more you do the inner work, the more you experience your own unconditional love, and you won't need it from others. A person who truly loves you wants you to feel free. A person who truly loves you wants you to have and experience the very best in life, even if it's not with them. True love expands, it frees, it releases, and it *actually* loves. You don't need anybody's love to fully be you. You are love. If you want love, the only place that you can get it is from you, from the universe, from nature, from inside. Everything else that you might be chasing is a distraction from the love that you are.

Chasing money is a distraction from the love that you are. Chasing security is a distraction from the love that you are. Chasing approval is a distraction from the love that you are. In the discovery and embodiment of the unconditional love and wholeness within you, all of that stops. You don't need anyone else to tell you that you're beautiful or handsome to know that within yourself. You don't need a job or a business to validate you. You don't need to mold yourself into the picture of success that this world has taught you in order to feel successful. *Your success should only be based on whether or not you are connected to the unconditional love that you are in this moment.* Success is not an achievement that you can hang on your wall; it's something that you embody moment to moment as you transcend the beliefs that say you should be chasing success somewhere else. Nature is never looking for a singular moment of success somewhere in the future; it's constantly embodying success as it moves into its next stage of expansion.

Eventually all of life will move back into the flow of nature. The control, the structures, and the manipulation on our planet is a result of a disconnected egoic mind that has shown up in the last couple of thousand years. It's unsustainable. It's temporary. It's an illusion. You can't control life. It's going to move and evolve and shift into something new. There are so many companies that are based on controlling and manipulating, and they eventually fall apart. They don't make it in the long run because they do not have a foundation-based flow with nature.

You can't manipulate the universe. You *can* manipulate someone who isn't connected to the truth of what they are, but you *can't* manipulate truth. If what someone is doing is against the expansion of life, it's going to collapse and fall back into balance.

We can't keep things the same. We can't keep life from moving forward. We can't stop life from moving through us. If you would clear out all that you're not to make room for what you actually are, you'll find that you'll always be rising, you'll always be moving forward, you'll always be discovering new opportunities and possibilities that show up for you at the moment you are ready for them. You start to move in a synchronistic way with life where you're effortlessly listening and noticing your next step in the moment and not stressing out about the uncertainty of the future. You start to trust that the future is unfolding perfectly for you. You're not looking for a future moment to be better than the moment that you're in right now, because you're connected to a universal love that is always with you.

If you want to move like nature, go into nature more, get silent more, release more, surrender more. If you want to move like society, which will fall apart at some point, stay on your phone more. Watch more TV and look for more approval from other people. Sacrifice your infinite connection to what you are for a job that pays the bills but drains your soul. Give your body things it doesn't want so you can distract yourself from your emotions. The more you let go of the societal things that are leading us into collapse, the more you'll get clear on what you are, the more you'll discover what it feels like to feel good for no reason. You'll join forces with nature instead of fighting against it.

That's my offering to you. Let those things go and allow your mental blocks to fall apart. Your love will catch you. Spend some time with yourself and learn to trust that you're taken care of once you stop fixing. Trust yourself. Allow yourself to love yourself. Let yourself feel and cry through all the layers of pain you've been holding on to. That pain is calling you toward love. That pain will transform into love. Wrap yourself in your own acceptance and watch all of your chasing fall away. You can see something bigger than who you've been. Go toward that. You're an amazing human who is capable of magic; don't spend your time living in the box that society has created for you. Learn what you are. Leap.

### Action: All I Need Is a Mirrorcle

*Okay, this one might feel a little awkward at first, but boy is it effective. Stare into a mirror, look yourself in the eyes, and stay there until you experience a shift where you connect to the unconditioned part of you. Do this until you can really feel the self-love that is underneath any of the judgment you might have for yourself. You are amazing. You are forgiveness. You are love. Look in that mirror for as long as it takes for you to find something that causes you to love yourself in a new way.*

CHAPTER 16

# UNLIMITED POSSIBILITY

I think you've pretty much got it now. You know, at least on some level, that you are an infinite creative being made out of pure unconditional love that doesn't need to do anything to prove yourself and that money is an illusion. One way you could take all of this is to just leave society behind and spend your days connecting with nature and gratitude and love. That would be pretty cool. If that's what you decide to do, that's awesome. What I think would be even cooler though, is to take all of what you have discovered about yourself and your relationship to money and leverage it so that you can create a massive impact on this planet.

If any part of this book has led you to believe that I don't want you to become extremely wealthy, let me tell you now, I want you to become extremely wealthy—if you desire that. I want you to live in your passion and allow aligned creativity to come through you so that you can create an incredible amount of abundance and influence in our society. I want you to connect with yourself in a way that gives you instant freedom from needing to do anything a certain way so that you can bring your unique essence into this world and be given back the value that you deserve.

The real power is beginning to move back into the hands of the people who are aligned with nature and the flow of life. This is a revolution that doesn't need guns or tanks or bombs. This is a revolution where an unbelievable amount of inspired creativity and innovation will flow into the world because of a deep connection to ourselves and the infinite creative beings that we truly are. This isn't one side against another; it's a revolution where everyone is invited to take part in accessing a new level of freedom within themselves that brings more abundance and harmony to the whole. We're not fighting against anyone. We're learning to love the fearful parts of ourselves and bringing our darkness into the light so that it can be released. The way that the world is right now isn't anyone's fault; it's a perfectly self-designed opportunity for humanity to rise above our limitations and step into the next dimension of our evolution. This is the greatest story ever created, and we're the creators of it.

I know that all the work you have done so far in this book will impact you and the people around you in so many ways—I have one last challenge where you'll get the opportunity to go way beyond your old story, step into something new, and cement this powerful vibration of freedom into place.

We've spent much of this process looking at a vision of what is possible in your life and identifying the things that are keeping you from that truth—this is an opportunity for you to take one final, spontaneous, and inspired action that will help you to transcend your habitual limitations and move toward what you want to create in your life. If your heart started beating a little bit faster reading those sentences, that means your soul wants to jump. This is your opportunity to act on that excitement.

The first part of this, which is easy, is to write down all the things that you think might still be standing in the way of a life of total abundance, fulfillment, and freedom. This could be a job, a relationship, a way of thinking, a belief about yourself. These would be things that are 1s and 2s and 3s on your list. These would be things that you say to yourself, like "I'm not smart enough" or "I don't have enough time/money/connections/etc." Write down everything that you are aware of that stops you from moving on your inspired ideas. Is it comparison to other people? Judgment from friends? Your own criticism of yourself? Spend a moment and do some housecleaning of all the ways that you block yourself from acting on or receiving possibilities in your life.

Now, spend some time writing down a vision of what life could be like for you. How much freedom could you have in your life? How good could you feel about yourself? How much love could you bring into the world? How much abundance could you receive? How many people could you impact? Write down the highest level of possibility that you can see for yourself, and experience what it would feel like for that to be your reality.

Okay, now, the second part of this is going to be where your opportunity to take a leap comes in. A leap is something that forces you to trust something bigger than yourself. A leap is something where you have to actually let go of the other side so that you can make it across. A leap is something that feels scary to your mind but exciting to your soul. So here's your opportunity to do something big:

Burn the list you just made.

I'm just kidding, that's not a leap, that's just a fire hazard with no actual change needed. Okay, here's the real leap . . .

Make a decision within yourself to do something for the next twenty-four hours that represents an entirely different vibration than the limiting things you wrote down and creates a new feeling of possibility within yourself. Remove everything that feels stagnant for you and move toward the vision of possibility that you wrote down. Prove to yourself that you are not just living in the wake of your limited awareness from yesterday. Go somewhere within yourself that you've never been for the next twenty-four hours and experience what it would be like to live inside your vision.

Call in sick to work, or better yet, tell the truth—tell your job you're going to spend the day finding what you actually are. If they have a problem with that, they don't support the highest you and you don't need them, so take the day off anyway. Go into nature. Take a day trip. Create a break in your pattern and spend some time with yourself doing something that you would do if all of those possibilities you wrote down for your future were happening right now. If you've got kids, take them with you. Spend the next twenty-four hours doing things that are a complete contradiction to the thoughts and circumstances that have been blocking you from acting on possibility and embodying the love that you are. You can start tomorrow morning if you want, or you can start right now and take a massive spontaneous action that rips you out of the stagnancy of your past.

If a belief that you don't have enough money has been blocking your possibility, take the day to indulge yourself in things that you haven't been giving yourself because of that belief. You don't have to buy a Ferrari on credit, just give yourself something nice that you've been denying yourself, like a day at the spa or a massage or a nice meal. If feelings of "not having enough" show up, just allow and bring them into the unconditional love and abundance that you are. Imagine that this level of abundance is normal for you and know that you deserve it. Pay attention throughout the day to any higher-level thoughts that come in because of your higher vibration.

If a lack of time has been blocking possibility in your life, take a leap and prove to yourself that you always have as much time as you need. Take the next twenty-four hours and don't do shit. Cancel your appointments. Turn off your phone. Take a bath. Notice how many of the things that you believed you "had" to get done can wait. They will get done, probably in an even more powerful or inspired way, once you have the space to see a higher solution. Or, if you've been unmotivated and relaxing a lot, make a commitment to get something done in the next twenty-four hours. Remember, you and Beyoncé both have the exact same amount of hours in the day— it's only awareness that allows more or less to get done during that time.

If a belief of unworthiness has been stopping you from acting on inspiration, take the day to connect to your worthiness. Spend the day getting quiet and discovering the proof of how inherently worthy you are: your beating heart, your breathing lungs, your consciousness. If you weren't worthy of receiving love and abundance and fulfillment, you wouldn't be here. You are worthy because you exist. Spend time with yourself remembering that.

Whatever the habitual thoughts or circumstances are that have been cutting you off from the possibilities that are available for you in your life, move in the opposite direction. Move toward what you desire in your life. Rewrite the story—for just twenty-four hours. Those twenty-four hours might be enough to show you a glimpse of the flow of life that will reveal itself when you're not blocking it. Then maybe you'll go another twenty-four hours, and then another, until it becomes your new habitual way of being.

Obviously, I can't force you to do this, and that's not the point. The point is that you have an opportunity right now to evolve, to move past your old story, to make a choice based off the new, exciting information that is coming through in this moment instead of the old circumstances that are simply the result of your past level of awareness. You have the opportunity to choose the excited feeling of possibility instead of a reason why you can't. There are no guarantees about what might happen if you follow that feeling, but I guarantee it won't be the same thing that happened yesterday. Even if yesterday was a decent day for you, don't you want to go *beyond*? Don't you want to really live? Don't you want to see what you're capable of and discover how good it can get? I know I do.

---

### Action: Before You Do That, Do This . . .

*Before you take your twenty-four-hour leap, I want to give you the opportunity to tap into the vibration of possibility and discover all the things that could go really well in the next twenty-four hours. Our nervous system has collected an insane amount of possibilities from our mind on how things could potentially go wrong—that's how most of us are used to thinking. We think about how we could ruin a blind date by talking too much about how amazing the band Chicago is, or how we might mess up an interview by throwing up on the desk because we ate Top Ramen for breakfast.*

*These negative possibilities are all things that are within the boundaries of your old story based on your past experience. In this exercise, you have the opportunity to go beyond the boundaries of your story and into a new, Top Ramen vomit–free level of possibility. (By the way, Top Ramen Vomit is a cool band name, if anyone is interested in putting something together.)*

*So write down at least one hundred possibilities of things that could go amazingly in these next twenty-four hours. Write down things that are way beyond what you usually let yourself see as possible. You can write down that it's possible for you to come up with a million-dollar idea in the next twenty-four hours. It's possible that you could meet a new best friend in the next twenty-four hours. It's possible that you could write the first five chapters of a best-selling book in the next twenty-four hours. All of those things are actually possible. Because you can see it in your mind, that means there is some avenue available where life can provide the energy, the information, and the inspiration to make all of those things happen. This exercise will help you become open to those possibilities and raise your awareness so that when a possibility shows up, you're on the right channel to notice and allow it into your experience.*

# CHAPTER 17

# GOING OFF
# THE DEEP END

You have done an amazing amount of work by reading this book. I want to take this moment to acknowledge you and your obvious intention to grow beyond the story of who you were yesterday. I know that many of the things that I wrote in this book may have been difficult for the limited part of you to hear, and that you may have had many moments of wanting to go back to the comfortable old story, but here you are. So congratulations. You are no longer under the illusion of money—mostly.

Stepping out of the illusion of money doesn't mean that you will instantly get rich, or that you are enlightened and don't need money anymore. It just means that you will more often see the places where an egoic concept of money is pulling you out of alignment with the infinite being that you are. It's now up to you to feel those moments fully and choose to move back into alignment with your truth. Reading this book was the easy part. Now you get to truly live in a way that honors the new awareness that has shown up in your body. If you don't, that's fine, too, but just so you know, you will likely experience more pain than before if you stay in limited old ways of being, because your awareness is now higher (like trying to put Windows 95 in an iPhone). You can't go back to what you used to know. You've taken the red pill. You've gone off the deep end.

I love when people say that phrase "They went off the deep end." I always think, "That's so much better than staying in the shallow end." As you do this work and make the changes in your life that your heart is calling you toward, you're moving out of the shallow experience of ignoring your emotions, chasing external circumstances, and numbing yourself with distractions. When you meditate, let go of heavy things, or answer the calling inside of you, you're moving into the deep end. There's scary stuff in the deep end, like sharks and electric eels and frustrated dolphins—plus difficult emotions and anger and challenges that cause you to stretch your identity. In the deep end you're meeting yourself fully. And even though there are some scary things there, there are amazing things too. Like starfish and buried treasure and Aquaman. Under many of your difficult emotions there is hurt, and under hurt there is sadness, and under sadness is love. There's love in the deep end. There's the depth of the ocean and all the magic that life has to offer.

Hopefully you have people in your life who are fully supportive of you and want you to grow into your highest self, but if there are people in your life who are scared of changes that you make and say things like "You've gone off the deep end," just know that that's code for "Your expansion is scary to me because it's forcing me to look at how I'm not living up to my potential. Keep going so I can have an excuse to step into what I truly am too."

The changes that you're making and the calling that you're stepping into isn't just for you anyway. The talents and gifts that you have, and the things that you create—they're not for you either. There is an infinite amount of flow that is dying for you to receive it so that it can change the lives of the people on this planet *through you*. Your growth is for the world. You are here to raise the consciousness of the planet. You are here for the expansion of the universe.

As you move forward and stay strong in your intention, it will start to become your instinct to move like nature instead of the stagnant story. You'll look to give before you try to receive and will become a massive space of receiving. You'll constantly be moving toward your 10s and releasing past addictive habits. You'll be present to the unlimited opportunities of this moment as you appreciate your past and let it go. Your consciousness will raise beyond the problems of the world, and you will become a source of real solutions for our future. You are a part of the evolution of this planet, and every time that you align with the calling of your soul instead of the fear of your mind, we all move closer to what we are meant to become.

It's a choice what you pay attention to. It's a choice how you move. It's a choice to consistently stay in this energy and listen to how you feel. This book was your trial membership to the gym; now you get to decide if you're going to sign up and actually go to the gym every day. I'm not saying that I'm trying to sell you another whole set of books like an *Encyclopedia Britannica* salesman—what I'm saying is, keep doing the work. Real change won't happen without consistency. There might be days where you can't see any obvious positive results, but in the long term, the results are exponential. The results of meditating and being with your emotions each day stack on themselves. The results of not being mentally attached to

THE ILLUSION OF MONEY

money create a freedom where inspired ideas worth millions can show up. The results of you doing this work will echo out into the world forever—you will never be able to understand the impact that even the smallest decisions you make have on others. Remember that you are part of the whole, not just some separate thing out on the edge. The more you release your mental chasing, the more you will relax into that knowing.

We're not on this planet to just consume and watch TV and complain about the government—*we're here to actually live.* We're here to live on the edge of our soul and co-create with the universe in a way that transcends our old story and moves us into a higher vision of ourselves. Eventually, you will discover a new dimension of yourself that is free of the limitations, that is free of the stories, that is free of the pain, that is free of the illusion that believes you are separate.

You are nothing but possibility, you are infinite flow, you are infinite freedom, and I am dying to co-create with you. Whether I meet you in person or not, I know that we work for the same boss. You and I are co-workers on this planet in the service of being a light for others and showing people how free they can truly be. We are in the service of letting the universe flow through us so that we can create a world together that is safe, loving, peaceful, abundant, and full of possibility.

You are amazing. Choose it. I dare you. It's really, really fun.

---

### Action: Read This Entire Book Again

*Read this entire book again.*

---

# ACKNOWLEDGMENTS

Christy Harden, thank you for being in the deepest inner work with me as we discover what is really true just by being in the room together. This is getting so fun. I love you. I am in honor of this moment with you, because it's all I have. I'm truly inspired by you.

Vivi Cease, I love you so much and am committed to my highest truth in honor of you. I have never known a love like this and it's humbling. You are growing so fast. It's hard not to attach to each day because each day with you is so unbelievably special. Let's go on a walk and see Moonstone and Ruby!

The two of you teach me to love fully. I am learning to connect to the ground because of you. Thank you.

Dan McKim, who helped me to write this book. You are a brilliant artist and an even better friend. Is there anything you can't do? It's an honor to collaborate with you.

Kari Geddes, it's so fun to create and grow with you. You inspire me every day. Way to stay in the room with all of it. You are an incredible space of love and listening.

I love you both. You have brought so much to this company and my life.

My brother Kevin Cease, a creative genius who can make you laugh really hard. To his wife, Ruthie Cease, and their kids, Liam Marvin and Logan Cease.

To my dad, Alan Cease. Thank you for creating and building incredible, impactful businesses right in front of me.

My incredible managers, Norm Aladjem and Sanaz Yamin, and my literary agent, Peter McGuigan. Thank you for believing in me.

To Barry Wind and Sandy Dixon. I can't imagine what it would be like to do what you do, and you do it really well.

Kara Hamilton, Lindsay Genevieve, Emilia Raukis, Jervais Dionne, and the rest of the EOL team. I am so honored to know you all.

To Sally Mason-Swaab, Reid Tracy, Patty Gift, and the entire Hay House team. It is so fun working with you.

My two best friends of close to thirty years. Thank you for being the most incredible friends while I constantly changed who I was. Through every single phase of my life, you two were always there and you always loved me, even when I didn't love myself.

Justin Ison, dude, I love you. I have probably laughed over a million times more because of our friendship. So much of my creativity, joy, and expansion is because of our connection.

Angie Matesky Ertel, thank you so much for always embodying light and love and holding the sweetest, most unconditional loving space for me since 6th grade. I am so lucky to have you in my life.

In memory of my mom, Nancy Cease. I miss you so much.

There are way too many people to thank. So, I am just going to say thank you to everyone.

Thank you for picking up this book and doing the inner work. You are making the world safer for Vivi. We thank you forever.

# ABOUT THE AUTHOR

After twenty-five years of achieving what he thought were his dreams of being a headlining touring comedian and actor, **Kyle Cease** suddenly discovered that the belief 'When something happens, I will be happy' is a complete lie. Following the calling of his heart, he decided to quit his stand-up career at its peak, and now – as a transformational comedian and *New York Times* bestselling author – he brings his one-of-a-kind wisdom to sold-out audiences in his Evolving Out Loud Live stage show and reaches millions online.

Kyle Cease has made more than a hundred different TV and movie appearances, including *10 Things I Hate About You, Not Another Teen Movie, Jimmy Kimmel Live!, The Late Late Show with Craig Ferguson, Chelsea Lately, The Martin Short Show, Comics Unleashed* and numerous VH1 shows. He has two #1 Comedy Central specials to his credit and, in 2009, Kyle earned the #1 ranking on Comedy Central's *Stand-up Showdown.* **www.kylecease.com**

# Hay House Titles of Related Interest

*YOU CAN HEAL YOUR LIFE, the movie,*
starring Louise Hay & Friends
(available as an online streaming video)
www.hayhouse.com/louise-movie

*THE SHIFT, the movie,*
starring Dr. Wayne W. Dyer
(available as an online streaming video)
www.hayhouse.com/the-shift-movie

▲▼▲

*HIGH PERFORMANCE HABITS: How Extraordinary People
Become That Way,* by Brendon Burchard

*IT'S NOT YOUR MONEY: How to Live Fully from Divine
Abundance,* by Tosha Silver

*LET YOUR FEARS MAKE YOU FIERCE: How to Turn
Common Obstacles into Seeds for Growth,* by Koya Webb

*THE UNIVERSE HAS YOUR BACK: Transform Fear to Faith,*
by Gabrielle Bernstein

*YOU BE YOU: Detox Your Life, Crush Your Limitations, and
Own Your Awesome,* by Drew Canole

All of the above are available at www.hayhouse.co.uk

▲▼▲

CONNECT WITH
# HAY HOUSE
ONLINE

🌐 hayhouse.co.uk    **f** @hayhouse

📷 @hayhouseuk    **🐦** @hayhouseuk

▶️ @hayhouseuk    ♪ @hayhouseuk

*Find out all about our latest books & card decks • Be the first
to know about exclusive discounts • Interact with our authors
in live broadcasts • Celebrate the cycle of the seasons with us
• Watch free videos from your favourite authors •
Connect with like-minded souls*

'*The gateways to wisdom and knowledge
are always open.*'

**Louise Hay**